# THE PROFESSION OF SALES

## ...Is For Sales Professionals!

### Les Lent

Coach & Trainer for True Sales Professionals

# The Profession Of Sales

Published by:
Les Lent
1024 2nd Street, #402
916-474-0163

www.LesLent.com
www.TheProfessionofSales.com

Original artwork created by and used with the permission of:
Gapingvoid Culture Design Group

ISBN: 978-0-578-54414-4

Cover artwork: Gapingvoid Culture Design Group
Cover and interior book layout: Meredith Lindsay | Mediamercantile.com

Every attempt has been made to source properly all quotes.
Printed in the United States of America

# THE PROFESSION OF SALES

LES LENT

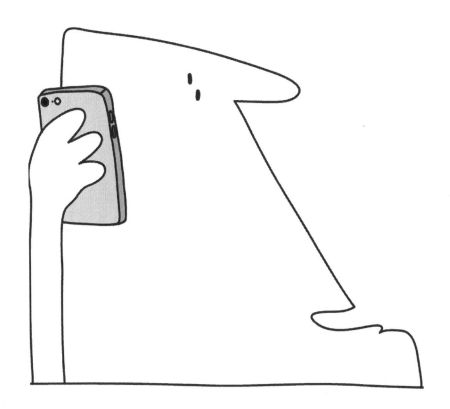

This book is dedicated to my friend and longtime mentor, Gerry Layo. Without his special brand of encouragement, this book would not have been possible. He will be missed but not soon forgotten.

# What People Are Saying

"Despite my 10 years in the VP of Sales role, rising revenue goals and a sales force who has "heard it all before" convinced me of the need to expand my management skillset.

I interviewed four consulting firms before engaging with Les Lent. His approach to sales is "real world," and the content is tailored to my company's specific needs, rather than the menu offerings of the also-ran consultants.

Les became part of the team—traveling in the field, speaking at sales meetings, attending a trade show, and holding trainings for the staff, along with our weekly one-to-ones.

We worked together for five months, did a full triage of our sales process, and put new procedures and metrics in place that will help me and my sales team achieve loftier goals without extended effort.

You never know what you don't know, unless you ask someone from the outside. I'm looking forward to continuing advisement with Les."

**—Paul Jaske,** VP of Sales, Aerogo

---

"When you get an opportunity in your professional sales journey to gracefully be taken to the next level, consider yourself lucky! I was selected as part of a corporate mentorship program to work with tenured sales coach Les Lent.

My goal was to become more socially present and push out my thought leadership more effectively. Les navigated me to unnerving nights of writing, posting, and being socially involved. I was able to experience true freedom to explore the areas of sales that I always felt could be impactful with a "safe place consultant."

Les guided me to new ways of thinking and connected me with valuable tools. I had immediate results, gaining larger followings, and was published immediately."

**—Erin Elliott,** VP of Business Development Allstate Roadside Services

"When the company was founded in 2013 sales were simpler—just find a few clients, deliver, and get paid. As the company grew, we started scratching our heads trying to figure out why our sales weren't growing at the pace that we needed.

The old ways weren't cutting it—what worked at a small scale would not work at a larger scale. Seeing sales slow down sent us into panic mode.

Les changed our whole sales process to accommodate customer demand and industry changes. He was effective immediately, creating a sales playbook. We went from winging it to having a plan that outlined the full sales process, from scoping to close. A huge highlight from the playbook is the call prep tool, which lays out how to be clear on calls and ensure there's a next step date and time.

As a result, our sales cycle was shortened from 90 to 60 days. Since inception we have closed our biggest accounts and attracted higher tier sales talent. We also engage in ongoing coaching.

Les is friendly, funny, conversational, and resourceful. He challenges status quo and is not shy to voice his opinion or speak up when others won't.

We are thrilled we've met Les and feel fortunate to have his expertise to help guide us to close key deals and take the company to the next level. I've learned so much in the first 12 months of working with him and look forward to learning more."

**—Henry Abenaim,** Founder & CEO CloudMyBiz, Inc.

---

I began working with Les Lent towards the end of 2015 and began a full engagement in 2016. We are a company who invests heavily in technology, infrastructure, and processes to support efficient and cost-effective distribution logistics.

After my initial meeting with Les, it was painfully apparent to me that our systematic approach to distribution logistics had not translated into our sales organization. We had successes, but we did not have a formalized, documented sales process. We also struggled with onboarding new sales representatives and getting them integrated into our sales system. It was difficult if not impossible to measure close ratios and duration of the sales cycle.

Les worked with us over two years and helped us completely dissect our sales process, identify areas of weakness, and formalize our sales program, which culminated in our Sales Playbook that is used daily by every GSG salesperson. In addition to the work Les did to help us formalize our sales processes, he has been instrumental in providing real-life field application-based training for our sales team.

Les has a unique way of communication with our team that provides them information and methods they can apply today. Les has been a tremendous asset to GSG and our sales team. Identify areas of weakness, and formalize our sales program, which culminated in our Sales Playbook that is used daily by every GSG salesperson. In addition to the work Les did to help us formalize our sales processes, he has been instrumental in providing real-life field application-based training for our sales team.

Les has a unique way of communication with our team that provides them information and methods they can apply today. Les has been a tremendous asset to GSG and our sales team.

**—Rodney Williams,** Executive Vice President Graphic Solutions Group, Inc.

# Contents

# Introduction

Maybe you started your professional life in sales, or you ended up in sales along the way because someone saw something in you and suggested it, or they offered you a job in sales. There are a lot of salespeople who were sold the job by their employer—the customer service rep or tech support associate so good at their job the leap to salesperson was a "no brainier." Regardless of how you got there you're probably reading this book because you're a hardworking salesperson who's looking to get better at your job, make more money, get promoted into management, or you crave the recognition that comes with sales excellence.

You've put in time, you've knocked on all the doors, followed up on every lead thrown your way, and you've even made it to a point where you can support yourself and see a future in this profession of ours, but, at the end of the day, you still want more. More closed deals, a higher closing rate, better clients, or membership in the coveted "Presidents Club" (or your company's version of it).

So, whether you're just starting out in sales, you've been in the game a while, an entrepreneur boot strapping a new venture, or you are a Sales Manager promoted from the ranks of the sales team and were given no process to lead by, this book was written for you.

As you digest the content, best practices and methodologies you may find yourself saying "I do that sometimes", or "I used to do that", or "I should start doing that" then you'll know you found a nugget or action item that will move you closer to your goal whatever that may be.

I hope you enjoy reading this as much as I enjoyed writing it.

## Success Through Process

My first attempt at sales was selling real estate, and it was a complete failure.

There were lots of reasons I failed—timing, location, no network, no financial safety net—but the real failure was completely in my control—no sales skills. I thought I was in the real estate business and focused all my energy and attention on learning that business, including real estate law, contracts, the marketplace, inventory, and so on.

It was no surprise to anyone that I lasted less than a year.

Fast-forward a few years later. ... I took another sales job in a different industry and enjoyed early success. Not because I had a better understanding of sales, but because I was in the right place at the right time and had become a subject matter expert.

As I headed into year two and my early success started to fade, I slowly started to realize that sales had a process of its own. My success would not be due to extensive product and industry knowledge—all my competitors had that! In fact, subject matter expertise is your prospect, customer or client's minimum expectation. In other words, they expect you to know your stuff! It's table stakes. So, my future success would have to come from understanding the sales process and becoming a student of sales.

I was fortunate enough to work for a company that was not afraid to spend money on sales training. Every quarter the firm would hire a "motivational speaker" to address the sales force and impart some words of wisdom. This typically happened on a Friday morning, while we were stressing out over customers and their missed delivery windows, product outages, credit issues and the like.

Most of the messages were entertaining but really had no staying power. I could not recall a single message from any of these motivational speakers that I could use the following Monday. Famed motivational speaker, Tony Robbins once said "Motivational speeches are like taking a warm bath. It feels good while you're in it, but the effects fade quickly." It wasn't until my firm hired my future friend and longtime mentor, Gerry Layo.

His opening remark was, *"I am not a motivational speaker, I am more of an irritational speaker, and I will prove it right now ... nobody wants to buy what you're selling!"*

This statement, when put into context of features versus benefits, resonated in a very meaningful way. He continued the training session by introducing us to his process outlined in his book *Smart Selling*.[1] Layo was entertaining, but more importantly he shared some very powerful ideas, tools, and processes that demystified the sales process.

Of all the things I heard Gerry say (and he said a lot through the years!), one of his initial messages struck a chord that stays with me to this day:

"The Profession of Sales is for Sales Professionals."

All became clear when I heard those words. If I were going to meet my financial goals, I needed to be a better salesperson, not a better subject matter expert.

This simple, yet profound message set me on a journey to become just that ... a Sales Professional. I have had the good fortune to speak, train, and coach countless Sales Professionals and Sales Leaders.

My goal with this book is to share what I have learned with you, the reader, to help you in your journey to becoming a Sales Professional. There is no shortage of benefits of being a Sales Professional versus a salesperson.

Sales Professionals earn more, get more referrals, and don't have to compete as much because they quickly differentiate and separate themselves from 80% of everyone else. Sales Professionals humbly know that until they do their job, nobody else in the company has one.

### Suspect, Prospect, Customer, Or Client?
Throughout this book, I will use several terms and words that may be inter-

rupted differently by different people. For the sake of clarity, I will define a few of the most important ones here.

*Suspects*, *Prospects*, *Customers*, and *Clients* may seem like the same people, but they are not.

A *Suspect* is a type of buyer—one you will encounter early in the sales cycle. I call these buyers Suspects because I *suspect* they might be able to do business with me.

The difference between *Suspects* and *Prospects* is this—a *Prospect* is someone who can buy from you! They are qualified, capable, and in need of your service or product. If they are not a qualified prospect you need to quickly, professionally and politely move on.

If you, or your company, have not done so already, there is tremendous value in defining and profiling your ideal customers—your best *Prospects*. A customer profile needs to list the industries you sell into, the title(s) of who is involved in the entire sales process, and their roles and responsibilities. In his book *Traction*, Geno Wickman outlines the three key factors in defining your target market: [2]

1. **Customer demographic** — What industry or industries do you sell into?

2. **Customer geographic** — What is your footprint?

3. **Customer psychographic** — What do *they* believe or think that make them an "ideal" client?

In my business, for example, my ideal client is a small- to mid-sized company selling products and or services B2B (Business to Business) with at least one sales manager and four outside sales people (demographic) in the US (geographic), whose leadership team is driven to meet their market potential and highly motivated to grow sales and profits (psychographic).

From there, you can start to capture the problems they face that your product or service solves, as well as the benefits they get by doing business with you.

*Customers* are first-time or one-time buyers. Depending on the nature of what you sell and to whom, you may only do business one time with someone.

That being said, I have yet to encounter an industry or business that sells to someone one time and only one time. I have worked with companies that make headstones for a living, and, yes, even they generate reoccurring sales with the same customers!

I have also worked with people who sell six-figure sail boats for a living. Nobody *needs* a 50-foot sailboat, but, when sold professionally, the first-time buyer can become a lifetime buyer or a *Client*. Fun fact, the average yacht owner will buy three boats in their lifetime.

*Clients* are the coveted buyers who buy from you and nobody but you, or at least mostly from you. They give you all or most of their business. Think of *Customers* as one-time, transactional buyers, and *Clients* as lifetime and loyal buyers. Most Sales Professionals have a growing list of repeat buyers that fall into the *Client* category.

While I will not go into detail about them in this book, there are two other levels of buyers to remember that usually show up on the classic sales and marketing loyalty ladders—*Advocates* and *Confidants*.

An *Advocate* is someone who will advocate on your behalf—someone who will refer you to others without hesitation. Many B2B decision makers start the buying process with a referral, asking for a suggestion from a trusted colleague when they need a product or service. To enjoy a long and successful career in sales, you'll need people advocating (referring) on your behalf.

At the top of the loyalty ladder are *Confidants*. A *Confidant* is that client who not only gives you all their business but also advocates on your behalf to others by providing you with referrals. They also see you as someone they can confide in when making tough or important decisions, even if those decisions do not involve your product or service.

A former client of mine who was in the office furniture business made becoming a confidante her mission. She worked tirelessly to become so valuable to her clients that, when they needed to purchase window coverings or carpeting, they came to her first—even though she did not sell either of those things.

I have been fortunate enough to have several of those types of clients and strive to develop more of them. Every great Sales Professional has a few, and those few can lead to a long and fruitful career in the profession of sales.

If you're ready to grow your sales to the next level and become a true Sales Professional, start by visiting www.TheProfessionofSales.com to take a free assessment that shows how your skills stack up now.

To your success,

Les Lent
Coach & Trainer For True Sales Professionals
Get More...with Les!
www.TheProfessionofSales.com
916-474-0163

# Chapter one

## Nobody Likes Salespeople—Not Even Salespeople!

Standing in front of a room full of salespeople at the start of a sales training session or program, I like to ask this question:

"When I say, 'sales' or 'sales rep,' what words come to mind?"

I typically get the same responses—sleazy, pushy, liars, and, my personal favorite, "salesy."

This is not even a real word, yet thanks to the online Urban Dictionary, everyone in the room knows what the word means:

> Salesy: an adjective for someone who is a cheesy, aggressive, and superficial salesperson of whatever product or service they are pitching.

I have asked this question countless times, and the responses rarely change—and this is from a room full of salespeople! I suspect the reason is we've all been on the buying end of a bad sales call.

If you have ever bought a car from a car dealer, you have probably had a bad experience. If someone has ever come to your door and tried to sell you magazines, you have likely had a bad sales experience. If one of your friends or family members has ever asked you to allow them to practice their multi-level marketing (MLM) business pitch on you, then you have most certainly had a bad sales experience.

The truth is, most salespeople are just not good at selling. This is not a formal accusation of them as people. It is a formal accusation of their ability to sell.

I don't blame them entirely, though. The problem is really systemic—bad or no process, poor or no formal training, little or no coaching from leadership and a lack of understanding how prospects, customers and clients buy.

### The Original Sales Approach

The result of having no process, no training or coaching leaves most salespeople to default to a system that is just not very effective, and, even worse, leads them to believe they should act and talk in a manner that is not reflective of who they really are.  It looks like this:

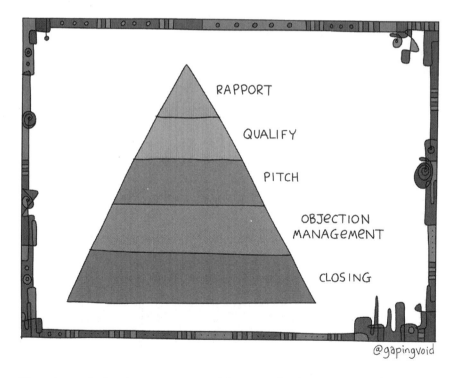

@gapingvoid

The sales cycle has five main steps. The typical salesperson will follow this model, either because they were taught it or they have experienced it before.

The salesperson starts at the top of the pyramid, and the size of that section is representative of the time and effort spent on that step in the process. So, as each section of the pyramid gets bigger moving from top to bottom, the typical salesperson spends more time, energy, and effort on that step of the sales cycle.

Incidentally, this model also frequently reflects sales management efforts as well.

## Step 1: Rapport
This is the step where salespeople tend to spend the least amount of time, energy, and effort—rapport building.

I am not a huge fan of the word rapport. Not because it is not a good word—it is, and not because it is not important in sales—it is! I struggle with the word because most people do not really know what it means.

> Rapport: A close and harmonious relationship in which the people or groups concerned understand each other's feelings or ideas and communicate well.

Rapport is an awesome word, and, yes, it does have a very important place in selling—just not at the beginning, and not the way most salespeople try and accomplish it.

Think about it. … Are buyers and sellers coordinated or in harmony at the beginning of a relationship?

No! You want their two most valuable resources, their time and money, and they don't want to give you either!

At the beginning of a seller/buyer relationship, there is no harmony. Most salespeople will try very quickly to establish rapport by making small talk or chit-chat, talking about the weather or last night's big game and so on.

We have all heard the story about the trophy deer head mounted on the office wall of the prospect. The salesperson, eager to develop rapport, asks,

*"Did you shoot that deer yourself?"* Asked in the effort to develop rapport, this benign question is how the sales call starts.

From the prospective buyer's point of view, however, this approach is typically unwelcome and creates a barrier and makes rapport even more elusive. When you do this, you sound like every other salesperson who has darkened their door.

Once the salesperson has checked the "rapport box," they move quickly to the next step.

### Step 2: Qualify

Qualifying is critically important in the sales process, but, unfortunately, like the word rapport, most salespeople misunderstand it. The typical salesperson thinks it means, "Can a prospect buy what I am selling?

If I am selling door-to-door and you have a door, you must be qualified. If I sell cars and you drive onto my lot in a car, you must be qualified. After all, we do not want to waste our time!

The typical salesperson will ask some rudimentary qualifying questions of the prospect like:

- *"What brings you in today?"*

- *"What are you looking for?"*

- *"When do you want to buy?"*

Once the salesperson has determined they have a "live one," they move to the next phase.

Of course, this isn't always the case. Many successful salespeople will use this phase to qualify a prospect using the BANT method. A simple and sometimes effective acronym to make sure they aren't wasting their time.

**B = Budget**

Does a prospect have the budget to buy your product or service? Is the money allocated? Is the money available?

I agree this is an important part of the qualifying process, but the most successful salespeople understand there is a difference between having a budget and having money. Said another way, just because the money for what you're selling isn't allocated to buy your product or service, that doesn't mean they don't have the money or can't afford it.

**A= Authority**

As with budget, I agree making sure you're talking to a decision maker is important; however, it is not the be-all-end-all to a successful sales cycle.

There are at least four people or personas, and you'll need to address throughout the sales cycle.

1. **Decision makers**—those people capable of actually making a decision.

2. **Influencers**—those people who can influence the decision one way or the other.

3. **Information gathers**—these people often appear in the form of gatekeeper (a term I detest!).

4. **End users**—these folks are the people that may have absolutely no say in the purchasing decision but will ultimately be the ones using your product or service.

My point here is you'll need to learn how to identify all of these personas to be effective in sales.

**N = Need**

Do prospects have a need? Said another way, do they need what I am selling? Needs can be defined at a higher level as pains, fears, or desires. If you're in a service industry, perhaps the NEED is to solve a problem.

**T= Timeline**

Are they ready to buy now? Are they in the "Window"?

## Step 3: The Pitch

Once a typical salesperson has checked the rapport and qualifying boxes, they move to this next step of the sales cycle—the one that gets the most attention when it comes to training. A clear majority of salespeople, and the companies they represent, feel this is the most impactful part of the sales cycle—the PITCH!

After all, every company has a story to tell about their company and its products or services. I call it the "Do" dance...

"Here's what we do, here's how long we've been doing it, here's where we do it, here's who else we have done it with, here's how much it will cost to do it."

Then when they have told the prospect everything they could need to know about their company, product, or service they ask, "So, you want to do it?"

Of course, they really don't say those words, but typically that is what they mean and what the customer hears when they go into pitch mode. The real words are more like this:

"[Insert company name] was founded in [insert year company was founded], by [insert founders name]. Today we are [insert amazing factoid, i.e. the nation's leading blah, blah, blah] ..."

Or...

"The Blah Company was founded in blah, by Mr. Blah. Over the past blah years, we have become the nation's leading provider of blah, blah and just this year we expanded into blah."

Most pitches start with the same language found on the company's "About Us" page on their website—seller and company-focused information—which leaves the prospect thinking to themselves, "*So what?*" or more accurately, "*So, what does that mean to me?*"

One of my first clients had a pitch book (they called it a presentation) they felt was essential to their sales process. When I asked why, I was told there were 17 benefit statements contained in the presentation.

Imagine 17 compelling reasons to buy!

So, they trained their sales team to memorize the pitch. They even had a condensed version ... the elevator pitch. You know the elevator pitch—the 30-second version of your story to tell someone in the time it takes to ride the elevator down to the lobby.

Another client, early in our engagement, asked if I would help them develop an elevator pitch for their sales team. I declined because I do not think anyone ever bought anything on an elevator.

If you are interested, the history of the elevator pitch is chronicled in Daniel Pink's outstanding book, *To Sell is Human.* [3]

I do think you should have a one- or two-sentence statement that answers the question, "*What do you do?*" and your answer should prompt them to say, "*Really, how do you do that?*"

My statement goes something like this: If someone asks me what I do, and I don't want to talk to them, I say, "*I'm a consultant.*" If I do want to talk to them, I say, "*I train and coach companies to greater sales and profits.*"

As a side note, it isn't uncommon for salespeople to pepper in little adjectives or statements in the qualifying process, too. I often hear statements like *"And another great thing about us…"* I can appreciate a salesperson being passionate and excited about their product or service; however, these types of statements typically are perceived as self-serving at best, and hyperbolic at worst.

## Step 4: Objection Management

In this step, the salesperson has finished telling the prospect how great it would be to do business with them and may attempt a trial close. Perhaps something like:

"So, you want to do it?"

Now it is the prospect's turn to talk. As I am sure you can guess, their likely response is not the coveted "yes" but some objection as to why they cannot or will not buy.

We all know the most common objections: Price is too high, happy with my current situation or supplier, bad experience with your company in the past, or just plain indifference.

Indifference means they do not see any difference between you and your competition or their current supplier or provider. And that is what every buyer has always been looking for…something different. I will address that more in a later chapter.

Now the salesperson shifts from presenting to defending their position and managing objections. As a side note to you, the reader—when you are buying, do you want your objections managed?

It is not uncommon for this portion of the sales cycle to turn into a tennis match. The buyer says, *"The price is too high,"* and the seller tries to manage the objection by reacting with something like *"What do you mean too high?"* or *"Compared to what?"* Or both.

The result is an unpleasant back-and-forth experience for both parties and most likely no sale.

The only sales training I received in my first sales job as a real estate agent was regarding objection management. They taught me a technique (let's call it a trick) called "reduce it to the ridiculous."

The technique goes like this: When a prospect says the price is too high, I determine what the delta is (the difference between what they think they can spend and what I want) and reduce that number to the lowest or most ridiculous number possible.

Let's say the mortgage on the house they want to buy is going to be $1,350 a month, but that is too high. They have a budget of $1,200 per month. The delta or difference is $150 per month. If I were to reduce that to the ridiculous it might sound like this.

"The difference between your budget and the monthly payment is only $150 per month. That breaks down to approximately $5 a day. Are you willing to lose the house of your dreams over $5.00 a day!?! That's like one cup of coffee at Starbucks!"

Ick! That is a horrible way to manage an objection. It is not only ineffective but also insulting to the buyer. And yet this is one of several objection management techniques taught to today's salespeople.

The objection process alone is worthy of its own book. And the best one out there is *Objections* by Jeb Blount.[4]

Now let's examine the last step in this antiquated pyramid sales model.

## Step 5: The Close
If you are in sales (why else would you be reading this?), you have heard the term ABC—Always Be Closing.

The last step in this sales model, and the step salespeople put the most amount of time energy and effort into, is in the close. They ask, plead, and occasionally beg for the business.

There are as many closing techniques as there are letters in the alphabet— probably more. There is the Puppy Dog Close, the Impending Doom Close, the Scales of Justice Close, the Ben Franklin Close, the Alternative Choice Close, and dozens of others. All of them are tactics and tricks not founded on anything of real substance or value to the buyer.

One of the worst closing questions of all time, and most frequently asked by salespeople, is this one:

"What's it gonna take to...?"

I say it is the worst because it is not even a closing question. At best it is a negotiating question. At its worse it's more of a statement telling the prospect, customer, or client that you do not have anything of real value to offer and you are desperate enough to do anything to get the deal done.

I observe dozens of salespeople making hundreds of sales calls every year as a sales coach, and I am always amazed at how frequently I hear this question come out—and to this day it has not worked.

## REALITY CHECK:
### It's Gonna Take More Than This!

A few years ago, I needed to get the oil changed in my car. The car was a lease and the lease purchase included free oil changes at the dealership.

When I arrived, the service manager greeted me and said I was in luck—they would be able to get to me right away and it would take only 45 minutes, as opposed to the normal half day window. So, I decided to wait in the showroom.

Making the short walk from the service department to the showroom, I saw a brand-new car that I really liked. I made the mistake of stopping to look at the window sticker and was immediately greeted by a salesperson. He was pleasant enough and showed me the features, speaking about the car's impressive safety and mileage. We went for a test drive, and now I was in play.

When we got back to the dealership, we played the game of pushing a price worksheet back and forth, doing the awful dance of "negotiating." Finally, in frustration, he asked *"What is it gonna take to get you to drive this car off the lot today?"*

I was just as frustrated, and my response was *"A better salesperson. Do you have one of those, because you aren't it!"*

To be clear, I want to say I'm a friend of all salespeople, even when I'm buying. This was the third car I picked up from the same dealership in less than four years, so I'm brand loyal, and dealership loyal. Let's not forget they know I am a legit buyer—this salesperson sold me the last car I bought there!

Full disclosure, I bought the car, not because it was a good deal but because I was emotionally invested—but it was the last time I bought that brand, let alone from that dealer.

Remembering the old sales model and knowing how ubiquitous it is, it's not difficult to see why salespeople get a bad rap! Far too many salespeople take this model too literally and don't pay attention to the subtle nuances of what it should really look like.

It's also a very tough way to make a living and is a prime reason behind why turnover with salespeople is so high.

And yet, this pyramid sales model is what you will be competing against most of the time. If you choose to follow this model, it will be difficult to differentiate yourself in competitive situations.

## Key Takeaways

- The traditional sales model is most commonly used because it requires little effort and even less thought.

- You cannot differentiate yourself from your competition if you sound like everyone else.

- If you follow this path, you will make yourself a commodity.

# Chapter two

## A Better Way To Work

Enter the Sales Professional. This is someone who is not just a subject matter expert but also knows the "profession of sales is for sales professionals."

They treat it seriously. They are prepared. They are engaged. They ask great questions and lots of them. And, most importantly, they listen.

Today's Sales Professional does not jump into the pitch or presentation. They know their real job is to discover and understand.

The key to the professional selling system, which I will go into further in the next chapter, is. ... **you must know what it is your prospect, customer, or client is trying to accomplish, and why it is important to them.** Without that information, at best you are a professional talker.

Let's look at a different and better model, one that is for Sales Professionals.

If you take a pyramid and invert it, again starting at the top of the pyramid and working your way to the bottom, you will see the first section is larger, with each section as you go towards the bottom getting smaller.

Like the original sales model from Chapter 1, the size of each section of the pyramid represents the amount of time energy and effort spent on that portion of the sales cycle.

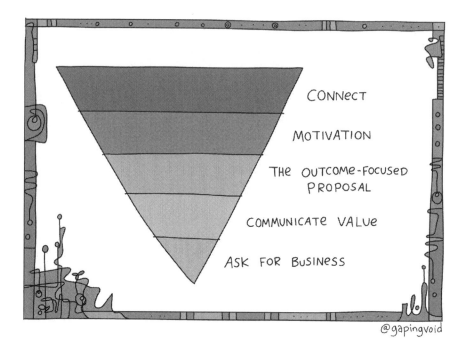

CONNECT

MOTIVATION

THE OUTCOME-FOCUSED PROPOSAL

COMMUNICATE VALUE

ASK FOR BUSINESS

@gapingvoid

### Step 1: Connect

In this first and most critical phase of the Sales Professional model, our goal is to connect with the prospect, customer, or client. Unlike the original sales model, which sought a superficial attempt at establishing rapport, by seeking to understand the person we are trying to do business with and their needs, we have a chance at connecting with them.

Rapport is the byproduct of a strong connection. So, as Sales Professionals, we need to be asking questions about them—about their role in the organization, what they are trying to accomplish, and why it is important to them. Given some thought, this will take more time and preparation than asking them about the weather or following the BANT method to the letter!

### Step 2: Motivation

Motivation means incentive to act (the "why"), or more literally, their motive to take action . In the second step of this new sales model, the Sales Professional's job is to determine what the prospect is trying to accomplish and why it is important to him/her.

Psychology tells us there are three main motivators in life and in business: *Pain*, *Fear*, and *Desire*.

*Pain* is the easiest to sell to. Pain is the suffering or discomfort a prospect may be experiencing, and they want it to go away right now.

*Fear* is a very powerful motivator, but it can also be paralyzing. Fear is the uncomfortable emotion caused by the belief that something is likely to cause pain. One of the most common fears is change.

The last motivator is *Desire*. Desire is their most wanted outcome. This is the "what" they are trying to accomplish.

Said another way, when you first engage with a prospect, customer, or client to discuss their needs, think in terms of their current situation, possibly pain or fear, and their desired situation.

Your job (assuming your company product or service is the right fit) is to help them bridge the gap from where they are today and where they want to be in the future. Like the first step in this model, the Sales Professional must ask questions and listen.

Not unlike a doctor, lawyer, or numerous other professionals, the Sales Professional's first job is to diagnose. This can't be done while you're talking, and it certainly can't be done while presenting.

The Sales Professional will spend the most time, energy, and effort on the first two steps of this model ... on discovery.

### Step 3: The Outcome-Focused Proposal
Once you, the Sales Professional, have connected with the buyer and have a clear understanding of their motives and most wanted outcomes, you don't have to pitch anymore.

And you don't need to spend as much time, energy, and effort on this step. Your job now is to sell them what they said they wanted and needed to buy.

Remember the pitch from the previous chapter? The 17 benefit statements contained in my client's "presentation"?

Nobody buys anything for 17 reasons! Most buyers buy for one, or two, or, at most, three reasons.

These reasons are typically emotional—they are supported later with logical reasons. You need to discover the motivation and emotion behind what they want and present that!

Said another way, discover what they want and need as an outcome and then focus your presentation on those things they value. Anchor the value proposition firmly in their minds.

## Step 4: Communicate Value

Unlike objection management, communicating value is about the buyer, or what they get because of doing business with you.

The absolute best Sales Professionals understand their customers require value and see purchasing decisions as investments. In this step of the sales cycle, it is critical to communicate the value and potential return on investment (ROI) the customer is making.

They still may push back and have some concerns and objections, but the better job you do at the front end, or at the top of the pyramid, the less likely you will have to handle objections. In fact, most of your objections, the really tough ones, will probably occur in the prospecting or lead generation phase.

More on that in a later chapter! The key here is doing a solid job early on to discover what the pain or fear is costing them and then show how your solution is less than that.

The same thing is true with desire. What is the impact on the customer's profitability if they achieve their most wanted outcome? Your product or service offering needs to be presented and viewed as an investment. Assuming the investment in doing business with you is less than the cost of continuing to be in pain or fear will provide them the return when they achieve their most wanted outcome.

The key here is to know what the costs of their pains, fears, and desires are and dollarize them.

## Step 5: Ask for the Business (or at least the next step)

When a deal should get done and doesn't, it's usually for one of two reasons:

1. The salesperson might have been talking to the wrong person, or

2. The salesperson did not ask for the sale, or next step, once they had earned the right to do so.

Asking for the next step in the sales process is crucial. Whether you are making your first call or the fifth in a series of calls necessary to move the prospect though your sales cycle, every call needs to end with a clear call to action or a move toward the next step.

In the antiquated sales model from Chapter 1, I mentioned the worst closing question of all time is: "*What's it gonna take...?*" The second worst closing question, short of not asking one at all, is: "*So, what do you think?*"

One of my early coaching clients had a sales model that brought highly qualified prospects to their offices for a presentation and customized a proposal based on the discovery of their need. They had a system of asking questions designed to learn what the client was trying to accomplish and ensure they had all the details correct. The entire process took about an hour.

After observing several of these sales calls, I noticed each one of the meetings ended the same way. After presenting a customized proposal tied to the customer's most wanted outcome and budget, the salesperson would awkwardly ask the question, "*So, what do you think?*"

The response from the prospect was always the same: *"We need to think about it, and we'll get back to you."*

Not once did a buyer ever say *"Yes, I want to buy this right now."* I asked the salesperson why they asked that question. Their response?

You guessed it! They did not want to be pushy!

I get it that nobody wants to be pushy (or any of those other words used to describe salespeople I mentioned earlier). The issue I have with this approach is, if you have done a good job asking questions and taking the prospect, customer, or client through the steps I just outlined, you have earned the right to ask them for the business—or at the very least, the logical next step.

When I ask a prospect what they think, when I should be asking for the business or asking them to take the next step, I am slowing down the entire process. When I say, *"So, what do you think?"* your reaction is to, well, think about it.

At the end of a sales call, I don't want you thinking anymore! Don't get me wrong—I do want my prospects, customers, and clients thinking during the previous four steps.

During the *Connect* phase, I want them thinking, *"Wow, nobody ever asked me that before."* During the Motivation phase, I want them thinking, *"I never really looked at my business that way before."* During the Outcome-Focused Proposition phase, I want them thinking, *"This is exactly what I need!"* During the Communication of Value phase, I want them thinking, *"I'd be crazy not to make this investment."*

When it comes time to ask for the business, however, I want to take the lead by asking one of the best closing questions of all time: *"So, what's our next step?"*

When you reach the conclusion of a sales call, the logical next step is some action or a step which will drive the process forward. Of course, knowing what the logical next step is in the process should make this a little easier. As an alternative to asking, "*So, what's our next step?*" you could say:

"So, based on our conversation, it seems like the logical next step should be... Do you agree?"

Another alternative might be. ...

"Do you see any reason not to move forward?"

If they say "no," then you are in fact going to move forward. If they say "yes," it doesn't mean you didn't get the sale; it means that you missed something earlier in the sales process.

It could mean you didn't connect with them as well as you could have. It could mean you didn't truly understand their motives. It could mean they didn't connect the dots during your *Anchor Value Proposition*.

By the way, if they don't understand your proposal, that is on you, not them!

It could also mean you didn't effectively communicate the value of your offering, or you sold them on the feature without connecting it to the benefit they will receive.

Whatever the reason, when you ask, "*Do you see any reason not to move forward?*" and they say "*Yes*," they are giving you the opportunity to go back and discover where things might have broken down.

This model, the model of the Sales Professional, is focused on the buyer and what they want to accomplish. The original sales pyramid model is really seller-focused, looking at rapport in terms of making a quick connection with someone so they can be moved through the sales process.

The Sales Professional model, while simple, is not easy, in that it will require thought and preparation. A model, which unlike the grind of the old sales model, can be the foundation of a very fruitful career.

## Key Takeaways

- Very little time, energy, and effort are spent on the buyer in the old sales pyramid model. Most of that process is seller-focused and self-serving.

- The Sales Professional model, with its upside-down pyramid, focuses time, energy, and effort on the buyer. It is buyer-centric and outwardly focused.

- This model, when executed correctly can differentiate you from 80% of your competitors!

# Chapter three

## The Two Must-Have Sales Skills

There are a number of skills required to become a true sales professional. Presentation skills, closing skills, negotiating skills, follow through skills, but the two must-have skills to be a true sales professional are questioning and listening.

Sounds simple, but it is not easy. It is not easy as it requires thought, preparation, and, of course, work. You must ask relevant, well-thought out, well-prepared, and well-practiced questions. That is only half the equation—the other half is listening.

Most salespeople get listening confused with waiting to talk, or even worse, waiting to interrupt. Your job, as a Sales Professional, is to listen with the intent to understand. There are two things you need to learn from any prospect, customer, or client:

1. **Understanding what they are trying to accomplish.**
   This is usually the logical reason they need to buy.

2. **Why it is important to them.** This is often the emotional reason they need or want to buy.

You will never discover those two things by talking, presenting or "pitching."

# REALITY CHECK:
## Know When To Say When

One of my first notable sales calls was early in my career. I had been at the job for about six months and was starting to feel confident about my new career.

This particular sales job was all-encompassing. It required me to open new accounts, service and penetrate existing accounts, provide consultative advice, and ensure account retention, just to name of few of the daily requirements. The job had a lot of moving parts.

As I got settled into the role and my new territory, my boss decided it was time to spend a day in the field with me. He gave me plenty of notice, and I was excited to get some feedback on how I was doing. I was also interested in impressing him.

To that end, I made sure we had a full and productive day scheduled. I had 10 calls scheduled, a mix of prospecting calls and regular calls on my active customers to get their weekly order and sell them new items. For each of my active customers, I had planned to sell them one new item they had never purchased before, as well as ask for a particular item they bought from my competition.

Eager to impress my boss, I had everything I needed for the day. Samples, marketing collateral—you name it, I had it.

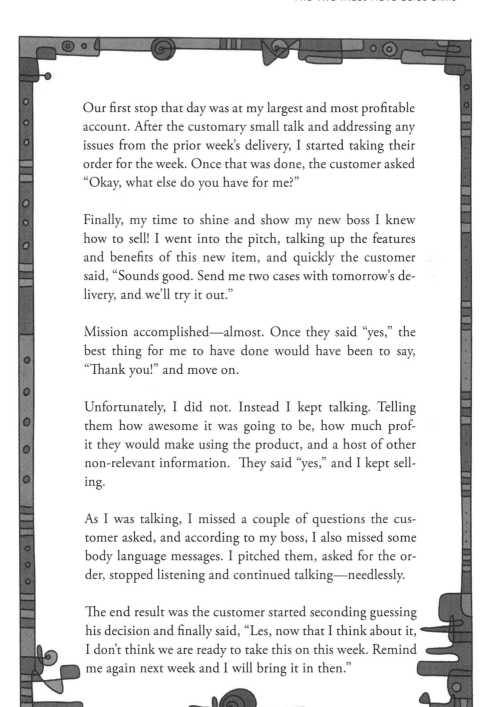

Our first stop that day was at my largest and most profitable account. After the customary small talk and addressing any issues from the prior week's delivery, I started taking their order for the week. Once that was done, the customer asked "Okay, what else do you have for me?"

Finally, my time to shine and show my new boss I knew how to sell! I went into the pitch, talking up the features and benefits of this new item, and quickly the customer said, "Sounds good. Send me two cases with tomorrow's delivery, and we'll try it out."

Mission accomplished—almost. Once they said "yes," the best thing for me to have done would have been to say, "Thank you!" and move on.

Unfortunately, I did not. Instead I kept talking. Telling them how awesome it was going to be, how much profit they would make using the product, and a host of other non-relevant information. They said "yes," and I kept selling.

As I was talking, I missed a couple of questions the customer asked, and according to my boss, I also missed some body language messages. I pitched them, asked for the order, stopped listening and continued talking—needlessly.

The end result was the customer started seconding guessing his decision and finally said, "Les, now that I think about it, I don't think we are ready to take this on this week. Remind me again next week and I will bring it in then."

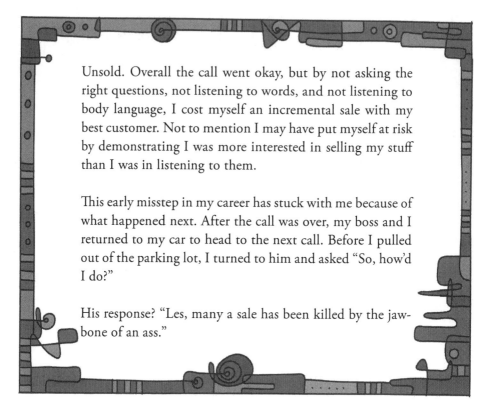

Unsold. Overall the call went okay, but by not asking the right questions, not listening to words, and not listening to body language, I cost myself an incremental sale with my best customer. Not to mention I may have put myself at risk by demonstrating I was more interested in selling my stuff than I was in listening to them.

This early misstep in my career has stuck with me because of what happened next. After the call was over, my boss and I returned to my car to head to the next call. Before I pulled out of the parking lot, I turned to him and asked "So, how'd I do?"

His response? "Les, many a sale has been killed by the jaw-bone of an ass."

## Choices, Choices, Choices

There is no shortage of sales processes out there. Go to any bookstore, and you will see a host of sales methodologies and books. There is *Action Selling, Agile Selling, Impact Selling, Benefit Selling, Spin Selling, Snap Selling, Guerilla Selling, Right Brain Selling, Whole Brain Selling, Ninja Selling, Samurai Selling* and tons more.

Don't get me wrong—those are all great books, and I have read them all and more. I am of the opinion, however, that there are only two types of selling that go on in the marketplace every day—professional selling and its opposite, amateur selling.

This is not to say that the majority of salespeople in today's marketplace are less than professional. But, based on my observations of countless sales calls, over 80% of the salespeople in today's market (and that is a generously low number) are selling, or trying to sell, in less than a professional manner.

They say the same things as everybody else. They ask the same bad questions as everybody else. They talk to the wrong people, just like everybody else. They jump to the pitch too early, just like everybody else. They bring up price too early and usually before the customer does, just like everybody else.

As a result, they look like, walk like, talk like, sound like, and act like everybody else they are competing with!

Today's buyer is looking for the same thing yesterday's buyer was looking for—something different. They are looking for a Sales Professional to eliminate their pain(s), mitigate their fear(s), and provide them with their most-wanted outcome(s).

Choices for today's buyer are at an all-time high. The Internet has given everyone access to everything. Fortunately for you, the Sales Professional, their expectations are at an all-time low.

They expect most salespeople will be bad. They expect salespeople will not follow up or follow through. They have come to expect salespeople will not listen, will not get it, and will not come through.

And they are right. Most salespeople will disappoint because they are amateurs at selling.

Professional selling is about connecting first, then discovering what and why is important to the buyer before quoting a price or providing a solution.

Today's Sales Professional knows how to ask great questions and how to listen with intent! Most salespeople don't ask great questions or listen well.

There are some salespeople who seemingly ask good questions, questions the buyer is forced to answer in terms of the seller, but they don't listen well. I call them "slick talkers."

There are also a few sellers who listen well, but don't ask a lot of questions. I guess you'd call them therapists!

In the chapters that follow, I will walk you through each of the steps from the Sales Professional Model in more detail, following the inverted pyramid diagram, so you can better understand this professional selling system.

---

Key Takeaways

- Two must-have sales skills are asking questions and listening.

- Sales Professionals don't allow themselves to be commodities.

---

# Chapter four

## Sell Like A Boy Scout!

The motto of the Boy Scouts of America is "be prepared."

That motto should be taken up by the Sales Professional as well. The number one area of dysfunction with your average salesperson is preparation, or rather a lack of preparation.

There are lots of reasons, including no clarity of what they are trying to accomplish on each sales call; no time to prepare (because they are too tied up working on unproductive things); and, the most dangerous reason of all— the notion that they can navigate through a sales call based on *their* product knowledge or expertise.

The problem with relying solely on being an expert is, in the mind of today's buyer, that it's table stakes. It is their minimum expectation that you know your stuff. They expect your competition knows their stuff, too!

Another problem with relying on your experience and intuition is that you wing it, or as I like to call it, "shooting from the lip."

This mentality of "I got this..." plays out far too often in the field. The problem is when you go in with little or no preparation, we are wasting everyone's time (our most valuable asset), bringing little or no value, and extending the sales cycle.

The client agreed to take your meeting because they have something they need or want. Your job, as a Sales Professional, is to get that out on the table.

Again, you can't do that by telling them all about you and your stuff; you need to ask about them and their stuff.

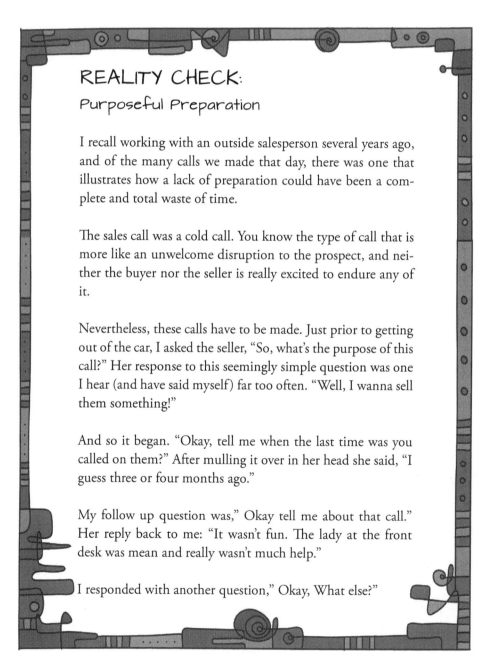

## REALITY CHECK:
### Purposeful Preparation

I recall working with an outside salesperson several years ago, and of the many calls we made that day, there was one that illustrates how a lack of preparation could have been a complete and total waste of time.

The sales call was a cold call. You know the type of call that is more like an unwelcome disruption to the prospect, and neither the buyer nor the seller is really excited to endure any of it.

Nevertheless, these calls have to be made. Just prior to getting out of the car, I asked the seller, "So, what's the purpose of this call?" Her response to this seemingly simple question was one I hear (and have said myself) far too often. "Well, I wanna sell them something!"

And so it began. "Okay, tell me when the last time was you called on them?" After mulling it over in her head she said, "I guess three or four months ago."

My follow up question was," Okay tell me about that call." Her reply back to me: "It wasn't fun. The lady at the front desk was mean and really wasn't much help."

I responded with another question," Okay, What else?"

And she answered, "I did learn they were getting a new purchasing manager, but they hadn't started yet."

"Do you have that person's name?" I asked. The look on her face told me the answer was "No."

Our discussion went on for a few more awkward minutes. … "Who do they buy from now?" I asked. Her reluctant response: "I don't really know."

At that moment, a delivery truck belonging to my client's competitor came from around the back of the building and drove off. It was like icing on a cake to the seller because, by this time, she had started to realize she wasn't well-prepared for this cold call.

I pressed on. "So we don't know the buyer's name, where they came from, or even how long they have been here, but you're going to sell them something?" I asked.

"Okay no, not today!" she answered, a little more than annoyed at this point.

"Now we're getting somewhere!" I said. "Because now we know the purpose of this call isn't to sell anything, so I can ask you again, 'What is the purpose of *this* call?'"

For the next several minutes we determined the real purpose of the call was to make an introduction if possible and discover as much as we could in an effort to make another call in the near future—one in which we could present more value.

## Four Simple Questions

You will not succeed in "selling something" without some level of preparation. You need a duplicable process for preparing for every sales call—a series of questions you need to ask and answer internally before the call to help navigate your prospect, customer, or client through the process of sharing their needs and motivations with you.

The preparation process starts with four simple questions you need to ask and answer before every sales call. The first time I heard Gerry Layo describe this process, I experienced a sales epiphany. The first question is:

"What is the purpose of this call?"

By *purpose* I mean what is it you are trying to uncover, discover, understand, learn, or get your customer to share? What is your call objective?

Simple enough, but as I said earlier, sometimes questions aren't always easy to answer.

At the time of writing this book, my favorite "purpose story" is being asked to meet a sales rep, who I was traveling with for the first time to provide them coaching, at a donut shop—not to get coffee and discuss the day ahead, but to get donuts to bring customers! That was the plan for the whole day.

In the interest of making the most of every sales call, and for the benefit of all involved (especially the customer), every sales call should have a clear purpose—a purpose so clear you can write it down. If you can't write it down, you don't have a clear purpose, so don't make the call.

If you write down the purpose of the call, and it sounds silly (like checking in or dropping off donuts), it is silly. Again, don't make the call. Your customers are not burdened with excessive amounts of free time, so make the most of your time and theirs by having a clear purpose to every call.

If you are struggling to define a clear purpose to your call, one that is not self-centered and "salesy," one that the prospect, customer, or client will see as having value, try asking these three additional questions internally to gain clarity on the purpose of your call.

### Question number two: What do I know?

What information is available to you about the person you want to meet with? About the company?

Information is everywhere! The prospect's website, LinkedIn profile, company social media platforms, your own CRM system—there is likely tribal knowledge among the people you work with, other customers, etc.

The point here is there is no reason or excuse for not doing some level of digging. One of the worst things you can do is ask a new prospect to tell you a little bit about *their* business. Capture this information, in writing and your CRM.

### Question number three: What do I need to know?

These are the pieces of information you don't know but need to discover to advance the sales process or move a one-time customer into a lifetime client. What do you need to know about the person? Their role in the organization? Other responsibilities? How their boss measures them? What they are trying to accomplish? Why it is important to them?

As an exercise, you could brainstorm with your manager or colleagues and create a "need-to-know list." You would be amazed how quickly that list can grow. It is the answer to the simple question of "*What do I need to know*" that serves as the foundation of creating the questions you will want to ask during your sales call.

### Question number four: What do I need them to share or admit to me?

What is it that, if a prospect shared it with you, could be solved or provided by your company's product or service? What is it do you need your prospect to admit or share with you that only you and your solution can address?

For example, in my world, I need to get a CEO to say or admit they don't get their share of the market, and the reason is because they don't think they have the right people doing the right things. My firm provides sales training, coaching, and consulting designed to grow sales and profits.

The reason I need them to say it is the same reason you need to get your prospect to say whatever "it" is for you ... If I say it or you say it, while it is still true, it has an agenda attached to it. But if your prospect says it or admits it, then it is a fact. If you can identify what "that" is, you can create questions to get them to share or admit it to you.

Asking and answering these three questions will provide you a clear picture of the purpose of your call—any call, for that matter.

**Tying It All Together**
Okay, you have asked and answered the three questions of what is known, what do I need and want to know, and what do I need to get them to share or admit?

Now let's go back to the purpose of the call. Once you are clear on the purpose of your call, the process of executing that sales call starts by writing it down.

As I mentioned earlier in this chapter, if you can't write down the purpose of your call, you don't have one! Once you have written down the purpose of your call and captured all your notes, you should start the call by stating its purpose.

It could sound something like this:

"Mr. Customer, thank you for taking my meeting today. The purpose of my call is..."

I get that this approach may feel uncomfortable, or even awkward. I can also assure you that, if you do this well, it won't feel that way to your prospect. In fact, the opposite is true. They will feel the process is more organized, professional, and focused on them.

Once you get the sales call started, you will want to ask your prepared questions as well as follow-up questions. To be clear, a productive sales call should be more of a dialogue than a monologue, more of a conversation than an interrogation.

Ask only one question at a time, and let the prospect answer your questions completely. Always consider asking a follow-up question such as, "*Why is that?*" or "*Can you tell me a little bit more about that?*" Understand that the more your prospect is talking, the closer they are to buying!

Once you have met the purpose of your call or reached your call objectives, you will want to wrap up the call following four steps:

1. **Repeat, Recap & Restate**
   This step is critical for the sales call. While the words *Repeat*, *Recap*, and *Restate* may seem similar, there is a distinct difference among the three.

   *Repeating* is exactly that—repeating verbatim exactly what the customer told you, specifically the main points from the meeting You 'll want to do this primarily to ensure you got the details correct.

   There is nothing worse than ending a sales call, going back to your office, starting to work on a project or proposal, only to realize several days or weeks later you missed some critical piece of information because you did not repeat back to them what they said.

   *Recapping* is summarizing all the things you heard the prospect say. This lets them know you heard them.

   *Restating* is that last part in the process of taking what your heard them say and restating it in other words. The ability to restate what they said in other words lets the prospect know you understand.

This subtle detail sets the true Sales Professional apart from ordinary and less effective salespeople. The difference between *repeating* and *restating* is the difference between hearing and understanding. It also demonstrates your ability to listen empathetically. We will discuss listening further in Chapter 6.

2. **Gain Agreement**

Once you are certain you have heard the prospect correctly and have demonstrated you understood them by restating the main points of the call, your next step is to gain agreement on what comes next.

I mentioned in Chapter 2 that the last section of the sales process is to ask for the business. This is where you do exactly that. While you may not yet be at a point to ask for the order, you should certainly ask for the next step, and set a date and time.

Never end a meeting or sales call without establishing a date and time for the next move.

Who is going to do what? When is it going to happen? As simple as this step seems, it is remarkable how frequently it gets missed or is left as being vague—as in, *"I'll follow up with you next week."*

When a sales call concludes with a vague statement, the likelihood of the buyer and seller connecting anytime soon is very low. Ask the question, *"So, what's our next step?"*

Once you've agreed on that, ask a follow-up question like *"Do you have your calendar available? Let's get that scheduled right now."*

Simple. Effective. Professional.

3. **Say Thank You**

   You have stated the purpose of your call, stayed true to it, met your call objectives, gained agreement on next steps date and time, and now you need to say, *"Thank you."*

   Again, this may sound granular or even elementary, but it gets missed too frequently. You need to say *"Thank you"* like you mean it, because you should, and you should say *"Thank you"* like it matters, because it does.

   Thank them in person and thank them in writing. Don't send just a thank-you email. Everyone does that! When warranted, consider sending a handwritten thank-you note, or a champion letter. I will discuss this in more detail in Chapter 10 on Follow Though.

4. **Know When To Leave**

   Finally, the very last step when conducting a sales call is to *leave!* It sounds funny, and you would be amazed at how many sales calls I have witnessed that went well, only to be derailed by a salesperson who did not know when to say "thank you" and leave.

   A client of mine, who is a regional manager, recently shared this story of a sales meeting she was invited to attend with the director of purchasing.

   They were meeting with a salesperson to look at a new software system. The sales call went well, and they both saw value in the system and were looking forward to taking the next steps. The purchasing director needed to excuse himself to attend another meeting just as the salesperson was wrapping up.

   As soon as the purchasing director left the room, the seller, for some reason, started the sales call all over again! He reexplained the benefits and repitched his services to my client, as if she did not hear the same thing 40 minutes earlier. He ended up "un-selling" the whole thing!

One of my mentors said to me early in my career, *"Be bright. Be brief. Be gone."* You need to know when you are done and when it's time to leave.

## A Few More Points To Ponder

As part of your pre-call preparation, there are other things to consider in addition to the purpose of the sales call, such as what you need to know and what you need them to admit or share.

These include, but are not limited to:

- *What do you need to pay attention to before, during, and after the call?*

- *What questions you need to be prepared to answer?*

- *What objection they might present?*

- *What case studies or samples you need to prepare?*

- *What the next step should be?*

And don't forget the "What if..." scenarios that we never plan for, but often encounter on sales calls. "What if's" are those seemingly random things that happen on sales calls that can derail a well-planned sales call.

Things like ... Maybe the customer agreed to give you an hour, and when you arrive, they tell you they only have 15 minutes. Or you arrive for the presentation meeting and see two of your competitors in the lobby eagerly waiting to present to the prospect as well. Or you planned on meeting with who you thought was the decision maker, and upon arriving, you are introduced to several other people from the organization at the last minute.

Are you prepared for those situations?

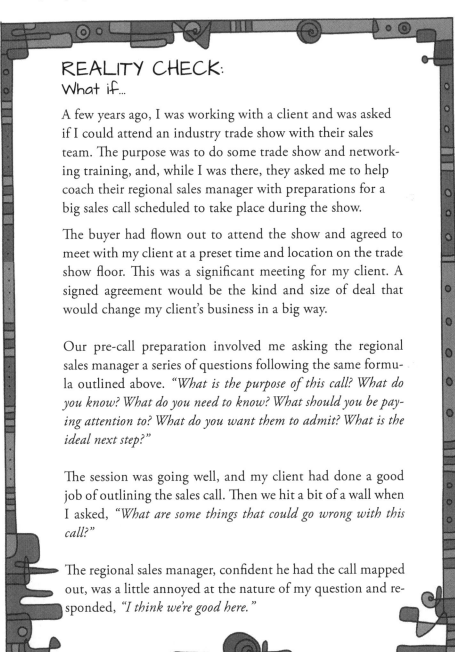

## REALITY CHECK:
### What if...

A few years ago, I was working with a client and was asked if I could attend an industry trade show with their sales team. The purpose was to do some trade show and networking training, and, while I was there, they asked me to help coach their regional sales manager with preparations for a big sales call scheduled to take place during the show.

The buyer had flown out to attend the show and agreed to meet with my client at a preset time and location on the trade show floor. This was a significant meeting for my client. A signed agreement would be the kind and size of deal that would change my client's business in a big way.

Our pre-call preparation involved me asking the regional sales manager a series of questions following the same formula outlined above. *"What is the purpose of this call? What do you know? What do you need to know? What should you be paying attention to? What do you want them to admit? What is the ideal next step?"*

The session was going well, and my client had done a good job of outlining the sales call. Then we hit a bit of a wall when I asked, *"What are some things that could go wrong with this call?"*

The regional sales manager, confident he had the call mapped out, was a little annoyed at the nature of my question and responded, *"I think we're good here."*

Knowing sales calls rarely go as planned, I pressed a bit more. *"What if he can't give you a full hour of his time? What if he can only give you a few minutes? What will you do then?"*

This, it turns out was the more than he could bear, and he became frustrated, saying *"You're overthinking this, Les. He flew out here to the trade show from across the country. We've had several conversations already, and he confirmed with me earlier this week. We're good!"*

*"Humor me."* I said, *"What if he only has 10 or 15 minutes? What will you do or say if he only gives you 10 or 15 minutes?"*

Realizing I wasn't going to let up, he finally gave in and told me what the three main points were and how he would communicate them effectively in a short period of time, as well as how he would alter his next steps in the unlikely event he only had 10 minutes.

As you can likely guess, when the moment finally arrived and my client met his prospect on the trade show floor, the prospect said, *"I am so sorry. I made an error in scheduling my return flight and I am not going to be able to meet with you for an hour. Can we reschedule for next month or do this over the phone?"*

Had my client not given some thought, even just a few minutes of thought, to the possibility this might happen, the deal would have likely died right there on the trade show floor.

## Key Takeaways

A well-planned an executed sales call has several parts to it:

- Write down the purpose of you call.

- State the purpose of your call.

- Stay true to the purpose of your call.

- When your call objectives have been met...

  » repeat, recap and restate the main points

  » gain agreement on next step(s), date and time

  » thank them

  » leave!

# Chapter five

## Want Better Answers? Ask Better Questions!

We've all heard the expression there's no such thing as a bad question. ... And I am sure everyone reading this would agree this isn't true—people ask bad questions all the time!

I remember asking a prospect, early in my sales career, *"What kept him up at night?"* I thought this open-ended question was what I was supposed to ask to get him to share his pain points. I thought this was how I was supposed to ask this type of question.

His response? *"My next-door neighbor's dog. Darn thing barks all night long!"*

### Bad Questions = Lousy Results

The problem with bad questions is they rarely result in good answers which are actually helpful.

In the sales process, I have heard all kinds of bad questions being asked by salespeople:

- *"Can you tell me a little bit about your business?"*

- *"What keeps you up at night?"*

- *"What would it take to earn your business?"*

All of these are bad questions because none of these questions require thought, and none of them are focused on the customer.

As a Sales Professional, your success in converting prospects into customers or clients is directly tied to your ability to ask great questions. Asking great questions benefits you and, more importantly, the customer!

Great questions will force the prospect to think. As you may recall from the earlier in the book, you want your customers to think. You want them thinking things like: *"That's a great question," "Wow, nobody's ever asked me that before," "I never looked at my business that way"* and so on.

The better your questions, the more comfortable you will make them feel answering them and the more open they will become. This leads to stronger connections and serves as the foundation for building rapport and trust.

Most salespeople think the more they are talking, the more they are in control of the conversation. In reality, the opposite is true—the person asking the best questions is in control.

The Sales Professional starts by knowing where he or she wants to take the conversation and asks a series of questions to get there. Every prospect, customer, and client you encounter in your career as a Sales Professional has a story to tell—a story about their business, their current situation, and their desired situation. To get the entire story, you will need to ask great questions.

It is difficult to sell to vague, wandering generalities. It is much easier to sell to meaningful specifics. To make matters worse, when people speak and think in vague, wandering generalities, it causes assumptions on everyone's part—I don't have to tell you where those lead!

When you are passionate and truly believe in your company, your product, and your service, it is easy to hang your hat on being a subject matter expert. As a result, salespeople are eager to tell their prospects what they know.

Unfortunately, most prospective customers, at least initially, are not interested in you and your knowledge or expertise. Your product or industry knowledge is a given early in the conversation. What your prospects are interested in is how you and your product or service is going to benefit them.

The best way to get your knowledge invited to the conversation is through the questions you ask.

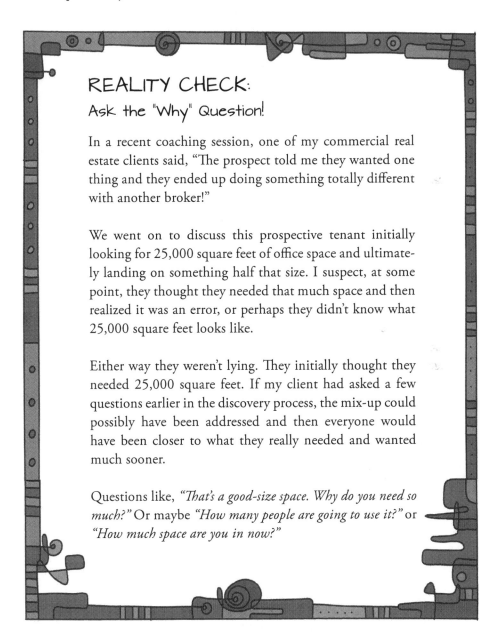

## REALITY CHECK:

### Ask the "Why" Question!

In a recent coaching session, one of my commercial real estate clients said, "The prospect told me they wanted one thing and they ended up doing something totally different with another broker!"

We went on to discuss this prospective tenant initially looking for 25,000 square feet of office space and ultimately landing on something half that size. I suspect, at some point, they thought they needed that much space and then realized it was an error, or perhaps they didn't know what 25,000 square feet looks like.

Either way they weren't lying. They initially thought they needed 25,000 square feet. If my client had asked a few questions earlier in the discovery process, the mix-up could possibly have been addressed and then everyone would have been closer to what they really needed and wanted much sooner.

Questions like, *"That's a good-size space. Why do you need so much?"* Or maybe *"How many people are going to use it?"* or *"How much space are you in now?"*

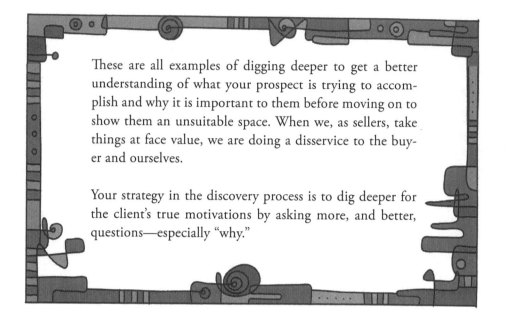

These are all examples of digging deeper to get a better understanding of what your prospect is trying to accomplish and why it is important to them before moving on to show them an unsuitable space. When we, as sellers, take things at face value, we are doing a disservice to the buyer and ourselves.

Your strategy in the discovery process is to dig deeper for the client's true motivations by asking more, and better, questions—especially "why."

## Questions In The Sales Process

For years, sales training programs have said you should ask only open-ended questions and not close-ended questions. While this is generally good advice, moving a prospect through your sales cycle requires more than just asking open-ended questions.

I advocate for asking questions in a manner designed to get the prospect to tell you their story and arm you with the information you need to present the right solution(s) and benefits. To help the prospect navigate the sales cycle, there are several types of questions you must ask. It will be critical to your success to plan your questions in a logical sequence.

### Connection Questions

These are questions about the person or the "who."

To be clear, these are not questions about the weather, their favorite sports team, or any other unimportant non-business-related information. There is a time and place for these more personal questions…after you have developed rapport, built trust, and moved your prospect through the sales cycle.

When developing your connection questions, think in terms of discovering who they are professionally, what motivates them, what they are trying to accomplish and why it is important to them. Examples of connection or "who" questions:

1. *What are their role(s) and responsibilities?*

2. *Where did they come from? (i.e., inside the organization or outside?)*

3. *How long have they been in the role?*

4. *What are they currently working on?*

5. *How is their performance measured?*

### Data Questions

These questions are the easiest to ask and answer. They typically revolve around the data or information the salesperson needs to actually do business with the prospect. As a result, this is where most salespeople start, and unfortunately stop.

These are the "what, where, when, and how" questions, as in *"What do you need?" "Where should it be delivered?" "When do you need it?" "How are you going to pay for it?"*

These types of questions are important, but they need to be in addition to the types of questions coming up below. Earlier in the book, I discussed the BANT method of sales—budget, authority, need, and timeline—and how many salespeople start and stop with these types of questions.

As I mentioned before, I don't necessarily have an issue with this, my issue is with starting and stopping at BANT and moving in the pitch.

### Motivation Questions

Motivation is defined as motive to act. It is the reason, willingness, and desire to do something. These are the all-important "why" questions.

Motivation questions are the questions you ask in the discovery or probing process. Your job as a Sales Professional is to discover, through the questions you ask, what your prospect's motivations to act are and why it is important to them.

Remember, there are three main motivators your prospect may have to act—*Pain*, *Fear*, and *Desire*.

*Pain* is the physical and/or financial discomfort your prospect may currently be feeling. There are numerous ways you can ask a prospect about their current pain.

*"What keeps you up at night?"* is a terrible question. Better pain questions focus on their current situation, such as:

- *What market do you struggle with the most?*

- *Why do you think that is?*

- *What is holding your company/region back?*

- *What are your organizational strengths and weakness?*

- *Where can you make the biggest improvements?*

- *If you could change one thing about your company, what would it be?*

- *How do you feel you can be more competitive in the current market?*

The second motivator is *Fear*. Fear is that unpleasant emotion caused by a belief that something or someone is going to cause pain in the future. Said another way, the pain is the real, physical, and immediate issue whereas fear is the feeling of imminent pain.

Fear is a very powerful emotion and can cause people not to act, even if they are in pain. The fear of the perceived possible pain is greater than the actual current pain.

There are all kinds of things prospects are afraid of—fear of missing out, fear of failure, fear of success, fear of change, fear of the unknown, and fear of you (sorry, but it is true)! During the discovery process, it is important you discover these fears. Without knowing it will be difficult to continue navigating the sales cycle.

Some examples of fear questions might include:

- *What is your plan to make your company's (insert specific) goal?*

- *What challenges are you facing in your business?*

- *Have you turned away any business recently?*

- *What is the biggest threat to your business?*

- *What are you competitors doing that you wish you were doing?*

- *What jobs do you dread?*

The third motivator is *Desire*. Desire is the prospect, customer, or client's most wanted outcome. It is their desired situation. This can be expressed in a goal, or even a mission statement.

While you would think prospects would be highly motivated by their desire or most wanted outcome, the reality is pain and fear are more powerful. Today's Sales Professional understands how important it is to uncover the prospect's desired situation. It is also critical to the follow through process, which I will discuss in Chapter 10.

Some examples of desire questions might include:

- *What product categories are the most profitable for your company?*

- *How do you measure success?*

- *As you look at your business today what are you excited about?*

- *What are your growth goals for the year?*

- *What does your ideal agency look like?*

- *Can you describe what a successful fiscal year would look like?*

### Gap or Deficit Questions

Gap or deficit questions are those questions designed to create a "gap" or "deficit" between what the prospect, customer, or client knows about your product or service and what you know about your product or service.

Earlier in the book, I discussed how the majority of salespeople rely heavily on their subject matter expertise, product, or industry knowledge in the sales cycle. The challenge with this approach to the prospect, customer, or client is that is can sound like a lecture if this is the crux of the dialogue.

Asking a good gap question will likely elicit a prospect to respond with something more like, *"What do you mean by that?"* or *"I never thought of it that way."* The point is, a good gap question will get your prospect to invite your expertise to the conversation.

The best gap questions are those questions that can be tied back to our earlier discussion about "what you need them to share or admit" in Chapter 4. In my world, I need to get my prospect (usually a CEO or owner) to admit something like:

"We have a great product and reputation, but I don't think we are meeting our market potential. I think the reason is because I don't know if I have the right salespeople and I don't know if they are doing the right things. ..."

During the discovery phase of the sales cycle, I have a much higher probability of moving them through my sales process if I can elicit that kind of information. Remember, I need to get them to admit this versus me telling them.

The reason is buy-in. If I say it to them, while it may be true, it is still suspect and has an agenda attached to it. If they say, admit, or share it through the questions I ask, then it is a fact, and they own it.

Working with the above example in mind, here are some of the gap questions I might ask:

- *Can you walk me though your current sales process?*

- *Other than revenue and gross profit, what sales metrics do you currently measure?*

- *What are the KPI or Key Performance Indicators for your sales team?*

- *Can you describe your current sales cycle and timelines in detail?*

- *What are your current sales metrics for...*

    a. *Number of prospects needed to create a customer?*

    b. *Lead to close ratio?*

The more of these questions that get answered with *"I don't know,"* the more gap I am creating and the closer I am getting to the prospect admitting they need help with their sales process.

## Follow Up Questions

Sales Professionals ask a lot of questions—almost six times more than the average salesperson. They communicate and don't turn those questions into an interrogation with their prospect, customers, and clients.

Many of the questions they ask are follow up questions to the answers they got from their last question. Throughout the sales process, the best Sales Professionals will dig deeper than ordinary salespeople. They digest the answer to their questions and determine whether they should ask a follow up question like *"Why is that?"* or *"Can you tell me a little bit more about that?"* or *"And then what happened?"*

Every prospect, customer or client has a story to tell. There is a beginning, a middle, and an end to their respective stories. Most salespeople stop when they have the bare minimum amount of information needed to get to the pitch.

I have witnessed a few Sales Professionals ask a few (maybe three) good questions and tease out of the prospect, customer, or client a bigger, broader and more detailed picture of what is really going on by asking a few follow up questions before moving on to the next question. Buyers will give you an amazing amount of information when they are afforded the opportunity.

### Closing, Next Steps, and Clarifying Questions
One of the best kept secrets in professional selling is the follow up question. I have already addressed this, but it bears repeating.

Advancing the sale and moving your prospect through the various steps requires you to ask them to take one step or several to get them to the end—a closed deal. We have discussed several steps, but it is important to know what the logical next steps are throughout your sales process and ask the prospect, customer, or client to take them.

It is difficult, if not impossible, to close a deal if you are not clear on what the next step(s) should be. If you do not know, how will they?

Clarifying questions go both ways. Throughout the sales process, you will want to ask them if they are clear or understand the nature of your questions, and you will periodically need to ask them questions to make sure you are clear on what they are saying.

One of the internal questions I mentioned earlier in the book that you need to answer is "What do I need to know?" The answer to this will serve as the basis for the questions you ask. To obtain more complete and useable answers, I have found it helpful to use probing verbs and phrases.

- *"Can you paint me a picture of…"*

- *"Can you walk me through…"*

- *"What does that look like?"*

This type of language encourages the prospect to give you more detail and a fuller, richer answer—an answer that may lead you to understanding their motivations and reasons to buy. The more they are talking and responding to your questions, the more likely they are to buy.

---

Key Takeaways

- The better the question, the better the answer.

- The better the answer, the better chance of positioning your value proposition.

- The power is in the probe!

---

# Chapter Six

## Listening—The Hardest Thing You Will Never Do!

Communication is one of the most difficult skills to master. Especially if you are a classically wired, people-oriented, extroverted salesperson who loves to talk!

Let's face it—90% of the time we are consumed with thoughts of our self and the other 10% of the time we are thinking, *"I wonder what other people are thinking about me?"*

Communication, in general, is challenging for many reasons. When two people are engaged in a conversation, there are really six people in the room. You have:

- *Who you think you are (your self-perception)*

- *Who they think they are (their self-perception)*

- *Who you think they are (your perception of them)*

- *Who they think you are (their perception of you)*

- *Who you really are (reality)*

- *Who they really are (more reality)*[5]

Additionally, most people are speaking under the influence. Not the influence of drugs or alcohol, but the influence of agendas and emotions. All this adds up to potential disconnect if the Sales Professional does not make a conscious and concerted effort to listen.

## The Six Levels Of Listening

There are six levels of listening, and we learn the first few at a very early age.

The first level of listening is *Ignoring*. This is exactly what it sounds like. One person is talking, and the other person is not listening. At all.

The next level of listening is *Pretending*. This is when one person is talking, and the other person is acting as if they're listening. It is usually accompanied by on-again, off-again eye contact, and when done well, the listener will make the occasional listening sound like *"Hmm"* or *"Really?"* The real pro at pretending will throw in the occasional head bob—I call these people "bobble heads."

The next level is *Selective* listening. We honed this type of listening as children, which is only hearing the things we want to hear. It's the *"Yes"* to our requests without hearing the terms and conditions that go with it. *"Yes, you can go outside and play...once you finish your homework."*

In the sales process, it's the language we selectively hear about people's interest in doing business with us or the buying signals the salesperson covets, without hearing what the prospect is truly trying to accomplish and why it is important to them. Either way, we don't get the complete story and lessen the likelihood of a favorable outcome for everyone.

As we gain more life experiences, our tendency to listen selectively morphs into *Biased* listening. This is listening to things while our brain applies our own finely tuned cognitive bias to the information we are taking in.

Cognitive bias is defined as a systemic pattern of deviation from normal or rationality in judgment. Individuals create their own "subjective social reality" from their perception of input. Said another way, we hear what we want and expect to hear based on our own personal biases.

So far, we have ignoring, pretending, selective, and biased listening. Obviously, none of these are effective. Yet this is the type of habitual listening most salespeople engage in.

The next level is *Active* listening. Just like it sounds, this is the type of listening in which you actively listening for thoughts, ideas, and facts. It requires preparation, desire, patience and, of course, asking the right questions. Most salespeople struggle to get this far, and when they do, they have a chance at becoming a Sales Professional.

The highest and most effective level of listening is *Empathetic* listening. Empathy is one of those frequently misunderstood, and consequently misused, words. The literal definition of the word is the ability to see through the eyes of another.[6] The deeper meaning is the ability to understand another person's point of view and the emotions behind their views.

It's just as important to know what empathy does *not* mean:

- *You must agree with them.*

- *They are right.*

- *You must like their point of view or belief.*

Empathy means you understand. Empathetic listening is one of the things that separate salespeople from Sales Professionals. It is their ability to truly UNDERSTAND the pains, fears, and desires of their prospects, customers and clients, their point of view and the reasons and emotions behind them.

The key to empathetic listening is knowing what prevents us from being good listeners in the first place. Things like thinking about what you want to say next or guessing what they are going to say next are two examples. When you do either of those things, you are engaged in your own thoughts and can't process what you are hearing. That's called multitasking and multitasking is a myth.

Multitasking is defined as doing two or more things simultaneously and correctly. For example, I hear people say *"I'm multitasking"* when I ask why they are scrolling through email while on a demo call with prospect.

There is empirical scientific evidence that humans can't multitask. What we are really doing is micro tasking and micro shifting. Meaning, we go back and forth between two tasks multiple times and are, in fact, degrading the quality of each task as we shift back and forth between tasks.

Said another way, when we are thinking about what we want to say next or guessing what they are going to say next, we are multitasking and are not physically capable of listening effectively at the same time.

Add to this our tendency to prejudge people. If you don't think you prejudge people, consider this—we are wired to prejudge people. It's in our reptilian brain and part of our DNA to assess people instantly based on a handful of factors.

We prejudge people based on...

- **Gender** *(male or female)*

- **Generation** *(Are they younger than me or older?)*

- **Ethnicity** *(Are they like me or are they different?)*

- **Education** *(Are they as smart as me?)*

- **Emotion** *(Are they more like Tigger or Eeyore?)*

Of course, the other person is doing the same thing!

We all do this in an instant without even realizing we do it. This almost-instantaneous prejudgment leads us to jump to conclusions and make assumptions. It is easy to understand why listening is so hard.

Another fatal habit that makes us bad listeners is talking over, interrupting or finishing other people's sentences. I was notorious for doing this early in my career.

These are the most common listening sins I've observed:

- *Multitasking*

- *Judging*

- *Assuming*

- *Thinking about what you want to say next*

- *Guessing what they are going to say next*

- *Interrupting*

Over the last several years, I have observed hundreds of salespeople doing the same thing—speaking when it is unwanted, unneeded or unnecessary. I call it "unselling" or "shooting from the lip."

Usually the salesperson means well. They feel they are contributing to the process, providing more information or answering questions and objections that have not been raised. They're excited about sharing the features and benefits of their product or service.

Of course, the problem with talking too much and not listening is that buyers feel they are not being heard. They don't or can't connect with you, your company, your product, or service. Often, they can't grasp the real benefit of your offering because they are overwhelmed with information and no time to process.

Oh, and they don't care about most of the stuff you are telling them. They care about what is in it for them.

I mentioned this earlier in the book, and it's worth sharing again what my first sales manager taught me, *"Many a sale has been killed by the jawbone of an ass."*

## Listening Empathetically

Now that we have discussed the barriers to being a good listener, let's dive into some methods for getting better at empathetic listening. First, here are some general rules of thumb:

- Look at the list above and ask yourself which of those bad listening habits you have and commit to stopping! While this may seem like an obvious solution, it's a lot harder than it seems. I teach this for a living, and I've been guilty of all of them.

- Prepare to listen by preparing for your call as outlined earlier in the book.

- Know what questions you need to ask, why you need to ask them, and how they might be answered. If you put more thought into this, you'll be better equipped to hear the right answer.

- Check for understanding by repeating, recapping and restating what you heard.

- Remove all distractions. Email, phones (if it's a face-to-face meeting), cell phone if you're on a landline, people coming in your office, etc.

Take at least a two second pause after the buyer has spoken before responding or speaking again. In that short space (it will seem like an eternity) of mentally counting, *"One, one thousand, two, one thousand"* ...the buyer will often share even more information.

An immediate response or reply can stall or shortchange a conversation. This happens all the time because one of the communicators (usually the salesperson) feels an immediate and overpowering need to fill any dead air.

Buyers are so used to being interrupted they seldom tell you the whole story. They will answer your question or provide insight about where they are within the sales cycle, but there is usually more they will share if prompted.

After a buyer shares something important, encourage them to tell you more. Asking this and other follow up questions can increase the likeliness of learning more.

Also, never (ever-ever) interrupt or talk over someone!

As obvious as this seems, it remains one of the most frequent transgressions in sales. In addition to being rude and putting you in a bad light, it disrupts the buyer's train of thought. Something important you need to know or learn will get missed.

**Practice, Practice, Practice!**
When you go through the pre-call preparation exercise, you will undoubtedly create some questions to ask throughout the sales call. To be a better listener, try going through the exercise of listing how they might answer each of your questions.

When you put thought into how they can potentially answer your questions, you will train yourself to be more aware of the possible answers. Even if you misjudge how they may answer, you will be listening for two or three possibilities based on your preparation. An incongruent answer is just as likely to be heard as an expected one.

"If we only listened with the same passion that we feel about wanting to be heard."

-- Harriet Lerner, Author & Psychologist

## Key Takeaways

- Only ask one question at a time.

- Give them time to process your question and formulate an answer.

- Repeat, recap or restate to make sure you heard correctly.

- To get to the "why" behind the answer, ask additional follow up questions before changing topics.

# Chapter Seven

## Sell Them What They Told You They Needed

So, you have successfully navigated through the early stages of the sales cycle with your prospect, customer, or client. You have made a strong connection, asked relevant, well-prepared questions about them. In return they shared with you, the Sales Professional, what they are trying to accomplish and why it is important to them.

You know what they want and need to buy! It is time to share with them how you, your company, and your product or service can help.

One of my early coaching clients believed that telling their prospects everything they could offer with all of the details of their solution was critical to the presentation process.

The issue was they had a lot of benefits and value propositions. Further complicating this was that buyers have one, two, or at the most, three compelling reasons to buy—and that's all they want to hear.

When you try and prop up your value by telling a prospect about features and benefits that don't address their immediate concerns, you run a real risk of disconnecting with them and likely will lose out to the Sales Professional who presents the one, two or three things the prospect said were most important.

### An Outcome-Focused Proposal

Let's go back to the Sales Professional Model for a minute.

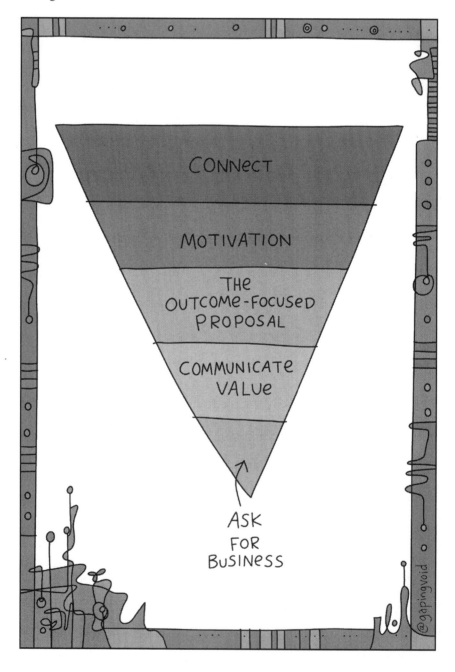

You see the proposal section is smaller than the either the Connection or Motivation sections. Remember that, when done correctly, you can spend less time on this step in the process.

To be clear, it does *not* mean you can wing your sales presentation, value proposition, or solution. Nor does it mean you do *not* need to prepare. It means you need to focus your proposal and its narrative around their most wanted outcome.

The reason you don't need to spend as much time on this step is because your job now is to sell them what they said they needed and wanted to buy. In Chapter 1, we discussed how, in the old sales model, salespeople are more inclined to do a data dump in the pitch phase and tell the prospect, customer, or client EVERYTHING they could need to know.

The challenge with this old model is the buyer can get lost in all the irrelevant details. Their solution or compelling reason to buy may be buried in the pitch, but if the details are surrounded by things only important to you as the seller, there is a strong likelihood it will be missed by the buyer.

Following the Sales Professional Model, you address the buyer's most wanted outcome with an *outcome-focused proposal*. You address how you, your company, and your product or service is going to deliver that outcome.

Said another way, just sell them what they said they need and want to buy.

Far too many salespeople get overly enthusiastic about their company, products, and solutions during this critical phase of the sales cycle. This over-the-top approach usually sounds like, *"And another great thing about us..."* or *"The great thing about us is..."* and, of course, *"But wait! There's more ... "*

Buyers buy for their own reasons, and they typically anchor their buying decisions to one, two or three reasons. Do you remember the example from earlier in the book where there was a pitch with 17 benefit statements? The prospect's one to three reasons to buy were buried in the presentation.

When things are buried, they are hard to see. Your proposal needs to be focused on their motivations, most wanted outcomes and perceived benefits, not yours!

## Features and Benefits

The most commonly misunderstood area of sales is the difference between features and benefits. The simplest explanation is *Features* are what something is or does. *Benefits* are what someone gets as a result of your product or service.

Your proposals and presentations need to be focused on the benefit or what the prospect, customer, or client gets as a result of ownership. You can address the features and connect how those features create the benefit, if necessary, but don't get trapped into the feature-focused data dump so many salespeople fall into.

The reason so many salespeople fall into this trap is twofold. First, most companies focus on training to their product or service—this requires rote memorization of the features. Second, it is easier to learn and memorize your stuff than it is to dig and probe to learn their stuff.

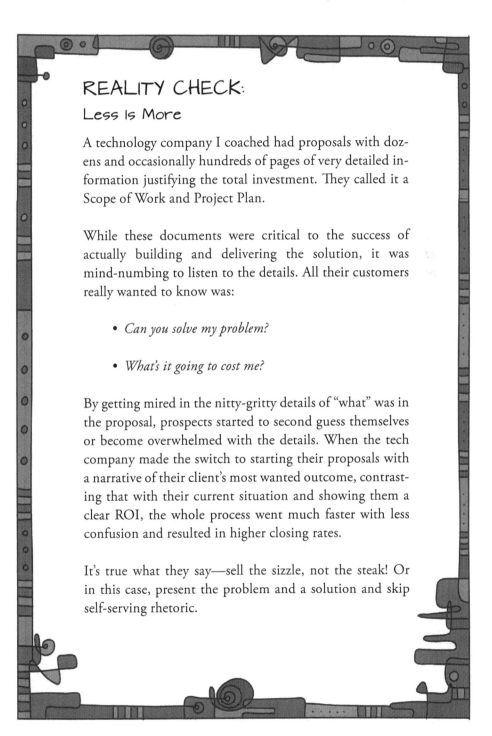

## REALITY CHECK:
### Less Is More

A technology company I coached had proposals with dozens and occasionally hundreds of pages of very detailed information justifying the total investment. They called it a Scope of Work and Project Plan.

While these documents were critical to the success of actually building and delivering the solution, it was mind-numbing to listen to the details. All their customers really wanted to know was:

- *Can you solve my problem?*

- *What's it going to cost me?*

By getting mired in the nitty-gritty details of "what" was in the proposal, prospects started to second guess themselves or become overwhelmed with the details. When the tech company made the switch to starting their proposals with a narrative of their client's most wanted outcome, contrasting that with their current situation and showing them a clear ROI, the whole process went much faster with less confusion and resulted in higher closing rates.

It's true what they say—sell the sizzle, not the steak! Or in this case, present the problem and a solution and skip self-serving rhetoric.

**It's My Turn to Talk!**

During the presentation or proposal phase of a sales cycle, it's easy to lose the prospect. When you as the Sales Professional are doing the presenting (talking), a buyer is looking only for things that resonate with them in your presentation.

If you go into present mode (telling) and the buyer doesn't connect the dots with your value proposition, it's unlikely you'll land the business. You cannot take for granted the prospect truly understands your proposal unless you ask along the way and help them connect the dots between your proposed solution and their need.

Imagine every time during your presentation you make a statement about yourself, your company and its products or service, the buyer is saying *"So what?"* You would likely stop the presentation to address that statement, right?

The truth is when you go into tell mode, this is exactly what the prospect is thinking! You say, *"Our firm is the industry leader in…"* or *"We are family-owned and vertically integrated…"* the buyer is thinking *"So what?"* They are really wondering, *"So, what does that mean to me?"*

To bridge this gap, you will need to tie the elements and benefits of your proposal to their most wanted outcomes. I've found one of the easiest ways to do this is by adding the phrase, *"and what that means to you is…"* to my benefit statement and close with what they get in return:

"Our company is vertically integrated (feature), and what that means to you is (bridging the gap) we control the quality of the product from start to finish and provide you with zero defects, and what that means to you is lowered build of material costs and higher profits (benefit)."

**Proposals, Bids, and Quotes**

Buyers and sellers use the words *bid*, *quote*, and *proposal* interchangeably, thinking they all mean the same thing. Nothing could be farther from the truth. Each has a unique meaning and place in sales.

A *quote* assumes the buyer knows exactly what they want and is looking for a price and nothing more. The prospect, customer, or client asks you for a price on a product or service. A *bid* is the same thing, except the buyer is asking multiple people for same thing. Both are recipes for low margin and no perceived value.

*Proposals* differ from bids and quotes in that they are solutions proposed to achieve specific results in exchange for an investment on the part of the buyer. Well-delivered proposals take the emphasis off price and place it on what the buyer gets for his/her investment, not what he/she will pay for what they get.

Buyers, prospects, customers, and clients can and will continue to call them quotes and bids, but Sales Professionals call them *Proposals, Anchored Value Propositions*, and *Outcome-Focused Proposals*.

---

## Key Takeaways

- Sell them what they said they wanted to buy.

- Make your presentation is about them not you.

---

# Chapter Eight

## Communicating The Value—What's In It For Them?

When I shadow a coaching client or listen to a recorded sales call for my clients, I am often struck by how open a prospect will be in sharing or admitting their problems, pains, fears and desires.

I am also struck by how infrequently salespeople will ask about the cost of the problem or the value of the solution. Said another way, how can you as a Sales Professional communicate the value of your proposal or solution if you don't know the cost of the prospect's problem?

The VP of sales of one of my clients sold a unique solution to a heavy problem—they sold equipment designed to easily move very heavy objects. They had few competitors offering similar solutions, and their biggest competition was the prospect sticking with the status quo.

The VP is passionate about their solution and the value to the buyer. He lives by the motto, "Solve, don't sell!" With thorough discovery and engagement with prospects to get the real cost of the problem and/or the value of the solution, he simply presents his solution as an investment.

*"So, Mr. Customer based on what I learned in the discovery process, you are struggling with the number of hours and people required to move this seven-ton piece of equipment through the various stages of production. You shared with me that, every time you move it, you spend $500 in labor, not including the time it takes away from production. In total you are spending about $1500 a day to move this equipment, or about $300,000 per year. Is that right?*

*With a one-time investment of $50,000 in our material handling equipment, we can lower that down to $25,000 a year in labor cost for an ROI of $225,000 in labor savings in the first year."*

The goal of your solution is to be more about money as an investment, then you can address the cost of their problem or the value of the solution.

### Reacting Vs. Responding

In the sales model detailed in Chapter 2, the second-to-last step in the process was described as *objection management*. The buyer, after hearing part or all of the pitch, or in response to a close or trial close, puts up an objection.

There are lots of reasons for this, such as they may be using the objection as a negotiating strategy or simply out of habit, or they may have misunderstood your proposal (your issue, not theirs). In many cases the objection is a request for more information so they can make an informed decision.

Again, in the traditional sales pyramid model, an untrained, wannabe professional will likely react. As human beings, we typically overreact to situations or words that trigger our emotions. For example, *"Your price is too high"* is universally accepted by most salespeople as being one of those phrases.

When we get into an emotional state, the likelihood we will *react* versus *respond* is very high. Those old-school objection response methods come across as "salesy" at best, and downright insulting at worst.

The Sales Professional model places a much higher emphasis on communicating value and recognizes it as critical to the sales process. The best way to communicate value is to start early through your discovery. Every problem, every solution, every pain, every fear, and every desire has a dollar value.

In his critically acclaimed book, *How to be a Rainmaker*, Jeffrey J. Fox devotes an entire chapter to what he calls "dollarizing." During the discovery process, it is important to gain a clear understanding of what things cost and what things are worth.[7]

What does the prospect's current pain cost them? Do they have a manu-facturing process incapable of meeting demand? What is the cost of those missed opportunities? Do they suffer downtime on the plant floor? What does that cost per hour, per day, per week? What are the missed opportu-nity costs?

If you have a solution to reduce or eliminate downtime or speed up pro-duction, what is that worth to them? The key to communicating value is to:

- *Know what your prospect, customer, or client's problems, pains and fears cost them.*

- *Know the value to them in dollars of your solution.*

- *Help them bridge the gap between the two.*

If your solution requires an investment of $100,000 dollars, and the cus-tomer's current pain, or fear, is valued at one million dollars, there is a clear return on the investment. You can't, however, communicate value in the ab-sence of this information.

You may feel uncomfortable asking questions tied to the financial picture of your prospect, customer, or client. But until you do get comfortable, some-one else will!

If you do your job in preparing your sales call, reviewing what you know and need to know and what you need them to share or admit, you can ask. Sometimes it's as simple as asking the question, *"What does that cost you?"*

If you build out the discovery portion of your sales call(s) and get them to tell you what the issues are, what their fears are and what their most want-ed outcome is, you will earn the right to ask, *"What does that cost you in … lost time, missed opportunities, wasted man hours, etc.?"* During the discovery process, there should be many opportunities to ask value questions.

If their problem or desired outcome is costing them more than the investment required by you to get their issue resolved or deliver their most wanted outcome, you have established what you are worth.

$$\$ \text{ cost of their problem or outcome} >$$
$$\$ \text{ Invest required by you for a solution}$$
$$= \text{Value}$$

When you communicate value, you are really asking the prospect to invest in you. When you do it correctly, they should see a clear return on the investment.

---

Key Takeaways

- Know the cost of their problem.

- Know the value of their most wanted outcome.

- Bridge the gap between those two things and the investment required to get them there.

---

# Chapter Nine

## Closing Is Just The Beginning!

I am not a big fan of the word *closing*. It has a connotation of ending something. A feeling of finality.

One of my favorite sales quotes is, *"Closing is the natural conclusion to a well-planned and executed sales call."*

For many of you, a prospect who buys something becomes a customer. When they buy repeatedly, they become, hopefully, a client.

Closing is a means to an end. Closing a sale, or closing the next step in a sales process, should signify something more. It's the beginning of a relationship, the start of a journey both you and your customer find mutually beneficial.

I have said many times in training sessions nobody wants to be closed. What I mean by this is that no one wants to feel manipulated or tricked into buying something by a smooth-talking salesperson.

There are plenty of closing tricks out there. You have the *Puppy Dog close*, the *Tie Down close*, the *Impending Doom close*, the *Ben Franklin close* and many, many more. Again, nobody wants to endure those tactics or tricks.

Jeffery Gitomer, in his classic sales book, *The Little Red Book of Selling*, says it well: "People don't like to be sold, but they love to buy."[8]

### Discover The Agenda

I was reminded recently by a CEO I worked with that he did, in fact, want to be closed.

What he meant was, if he agreed to take a meeting with a Sales Professional, he did have an expectation that the professional close the deal! If he was willing to invest his time and energy on a meeting, he had an expectation of moving forward, assuming they agree to meet with you, they have an agenda. Your job is to discover the agenda, what they are trying to accomplish and why it is important to them, and to move the sales process forward to its logical conclusion, helping the buyer accomplish their agenda—a closed deal! In his excellent book, *The Lost Art of Closing*, Anthony Iannarino takes this topic to the next level, buy detailing the 10 commitments that realy drive sales.[9]

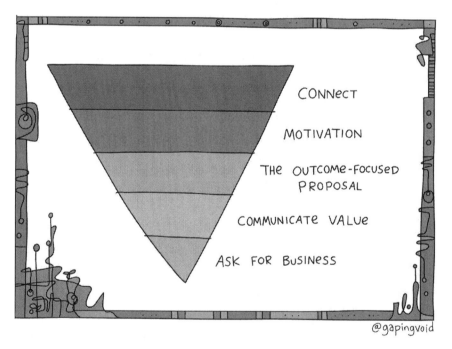

@gapingvoid

### Close The Sale (Or Take The Next Step)

Closing, or asking for the business, is really a transition from one phase of the sales cycle to the next. Whether you have a product or service that can be closed in one call, or a sophisticated solution requiring multiple steps and sales calls along the way, every step needs to have a clear call to action or next step.

Said another way, every sales call should end with something that happens next. That something is "the close."

As a sales coach, I have now observed too many sales calls to count, and that number would include the number of sales calls I have been a part of as a buyer. I've seen sales calls attempted to be closed using one of the following three methods (This doesn't include the calls that ended with no attempt to close and the salesperson hoping at the end the customer will make the first move unprompted).

1. **They are passive.**
   I define being passive as moving through the sales cycle, regardless of how well it's going, getting to the end and not asking for the business or the next step. Or asking in a passive manner.

   Let's say you did a great job throughout the sales cycle. You qualified your prospect, you connected with them, you discovered their pains, fears, and desires. Then you present your product or service as an Outcome Focused Proposal—a proposal focused on their most wanted outcome.

   So, you communicated the value and overcame any objections. Then, instead of asking for the business with a well-prepared closing question, you ask "So, do you have any questions"? or worse, "So, what do you think"?

   This is passive! You earned the right and didn't ask for the business.

   This is the number one reason a sale doesn't get made. The seller, whether they have earned the right or not, fails to ask for the business or specific next step in the sales process. This has the additional adverse impact of making it very difficult to follow though later in the sales process.

2. **They are aggressive.**
   This is the close that gives Sales Professionals a bad rap. The seller asks too soon (no transfer of trust), they ask too many times (pushy), or they say something like, "So, what's it gonna take to get you into this baby today"? (lame).

   Aggressive is asking for the business in less than a professional manner before you have earned the right. As a side note, "What's it gonna take...?" is not even a true closing question. At best, it's a negation question, and, at worst, it sends the message that you as the seller are not very good at connecting, discovering motivations, presenting value, or communicating value.

   In other words, you're an average salesperson, just like everybody else.

3. **They are assertive.**
   Assertive lives between passive and aggressive. You qualified, connected, uncovered motivation, presented, and communicated value. Once these steps are completed, you have earned the right to ask in an assertive fashion. You ask your prospect something like, "Do you see any reason we shouldn't move forward?" or "So, what's our next step?"

   In general, well-prepared Sales Professionals don't ask but tell their prospects what the next step should be. "Based on everything we've discussed, it seems like the logical next step would be..." This level of preparation is what separates the most successful Sales Professionals from the majority of salespeople.

So, which type of closer are you going to be?

## Key Takeaways

- Know what the most logical next step should be as part of your pre-call planning.

- Ask for the next step once you have earned the right.

# Chapter Ten

## Follow Through Is *Your* Job, Not Theirs

My first job as a sales manager was tough, and those experiences are worthy of another book.

One of the most frustrating things I ever experienced was a new prospective business being built in my territory. This was a ground floor opportunity and we wanted it.

Every week one of my reps would report on prospecting the account and state they had called and left a message, sent an email, or "stopped by" and dropped off some marketing material. Weeks of this.

**Me:** *"Did you follow up with so-and-so?"*

**Them:** *"Yes I followed up. I left them a message."* Or *"Yes, I stopped by."*

Lots of activity but little or no productivity. After several weeks of "following up," we ultimately lost the business to a competitor that actually followed through.

### Follow Through Vs. Follow Up

Follow up is a struggle for many salespeople and sales managers.

For the seller, the struggle is usually in reconnecting with the prospect, customer, or client after the last meeting. Perhaps there was no call to action or clear next step, date, and time set at the end of the last meeting. Or, worse yet, the prospect was underwhelmed and not interested in moving forward.

The other reason salespeople struggle with follow up is a lack of something of value to say. Having nothing else to say, the seller leaves voicemails and emails like this, *"I'm just following up with you…"* No value and, as a result, no connection.

For sales managers, the struggle is a little different. Managing an opportunity pipeline, they meet with their sales team and ask for status updates on specific opportunities in CRM. *"Where are we with so-and-so? Have you followed up?"* The salesperson, having sent an email and left a voicemail, can respond, *"Yes, I left them a message, but I haven't heard back."*

A merry go-round of no progress!

The difference between *follow up* and *follow through* starts with an attitude of knowing the prospect, customer or client isn't responsible for reconnecting with you just because you "pinged" them.

It's also important to recognize they have other responsibilities in their role. This one hurts, but they usually stop thinking about you as soon as the last interaction ended. They aren't sitting around thinking about buying your stuff. They have moved on to the next priority.

*Follow up* is an attitude of engaging in an activity of leaving the customer to take the next step by hoping they return *your* call or respond to *your* email. It is an incomplete process.

*Follow through* is when you reconnect and have the next conversation necessary to advance a prospect into or though the sales cycle. To use a sports analogy, no baseball, football, or basketball coach ever shouted, *"Follow up with the ball!"* They shouted, *"Follow through with the ball!"*

You need to complete the motion in sports, or in sales, the next step in the process. Let's look at some different kinds of follow through.

### Types of Follow Through
There are three types of follow through with a prospect, customer, or client.

The first type is to advance someone in your sales cycle to the next step in your process. For example, they had a product demo, and the next step is to present a proposal. Your follow through takes them to the next step.

The second type of follow through is when a prospect requests some information or reaches out to you. Perhaps they saw an ad, or they are responding to your company's marketing efforts.

They are in play! The Sales Professional has a sense of urgency and responds quickly and professionally until they have connected. The sales manager knows the true cost of a marketing-generated lead and the value of converting the lead to revenue.

The third type of follow through is one that nurtures a prospect into entering your sales process at some point in the future. This type takes consistency and value.

Today's Sales Professional understands *how* they follow through with their prospects says more about them and their personal brand than all the company's marketing collateral combined.

Examples of this type of follow through can include sending whitepapers, handwritten thank-you cards, and value-added content through newsletters or sharing pertinent and timely information with a prospect. The goal is to stay top-of-mind with the prospect so when they are ready, they think of you first.

Today's Sales Professional knows follow through is not the customer's job! Far too many salespeople think once they respond to an inquiry generated by marketing (usually by email or voicemail) or try to re-engage a prospect after the last meeting, the ball is now in the prospect's court. They put the burden of taking the next step back into the prospect's hands, believing the prospect or customer will act.

Think about this for a minute. ... Put yourself in the buyer's shoes. They have other stuff to do, like work and life. What else might they be dealing with besides trying to buy your stuff? What other priorities might they have?

You may need to reach out multiple times before you go from first contact to signed contract. More than 48% of sellers will make just one attempt to connect with a prospect and then give up. I call them "one-hit wonders." They hit the prospect one time, then wonder where the business went.

Prospects and buyers have low expectations of today's salespeople and customer service reps. Think of a company you *love* to do business with and why. Now think of a company you *hate* to do business with and why.

The answer to the second question came easier, faster and had more detail, didn't it? Numerous unpleasant consumer experiences have conditioned us to expect the very minimum effort.

Prospects have more choices and information than ever before. That means they will not wait around very long for you to get back to them with the information needed or requested. If your website and social media campaigns could answer all their questions, they would not have called you.

So, your customer goes to the next result from a web search, and the next guy gets a shot. Riding on the coattails of your well-spent SEO dollars. First call back wins!

Can you say, "jump ball"?

### Strategies for Effective Follow Through
Regardless of what you sell, there are some basic skills you MUST have as a Sales Professional. Pre-call planning, asking questions, listening, and presenting are all critical to producing revenue-generating events for your company.

Of all the things today's Sales Professional should do, follow through is key. Here are some of the must-have areas you need to have covered:

1. **Know Your Job**

   Marketing makes the promise via marketing campaigns to create visibility. How you follow through makes your marketing department (and your company) look like heroes or liars. Follow through, along with pre-call preparation and execution, is the life of a Sales Professional, and you need to be responsible for it.

2. **Planning and Persistence**

   If you cannot make contact, you lose! Call, email, send hand-written "thank you" cards. Give multiple touches and multiple messages and have something to say.

   As a side note, you must prepare for the conversation you plan to have on the phone, and you should plan the message you leave in the event you get their voicemail—at least if you want them to call you back.

   Many of you may be wondering how many times you should attempt to connect before giving up? Never give up! If you do admit defeat, make at least eight touches first.

3. **No Schedule, No Commitment**

   Follow through is a huge part of your job as a sales professional; in fact, it is number two on the list where most salespeople come up short!

   Follow through needs to be on your calendar, not just your to-do list. Otherwise, it will go from the bottom of your to-do list to the top of your to-don't list. Make it a priority and schedule blocks of time to conduct follow- through calls (activities).

   Many people find it easiest to schedule follow throughs throughout the day. You could carve out three, 30-minute blocks for morning, afternoon, and end of day. And yes, put it on your calendar! Create a follow through habit.

As a sales professional, consider creating a personal mission statement about how you follow through—something like *"Return every call every day."* My follow through statement is, *"I will return your call or respond to your email within 24 hours or by the end of the next business day, whichever comes first."*

So ... how, when and with what frequency are you going to follow through with your prospects, customers, and clients?

## The Impact of Saying Thank You

I have recently been reminded, several times, just how important handwritten thank-you notes can be in the business world.

When I work with sales professionals as a coach, or when I meet someone new and start to build a relationship, I send them a short, handwritten thank you card. Nothing extravagant—just a brief note thanking them for something specific (usually their time).

I have made it a habit—I carry a small bag in my brief case with note cards, envelopes, business cards and a pen. I don't take for granted the positive effect of these gestures, but I do sometimes wonder how they are received.

I got a thank-you card from the Chairman of the Board of one of my clients. It was a note saying, *"Thank you"* for my efforts and stating his support. It was only two sentences, but they had a big impact!

## Law of Reciprocity

One of the reasons handwritten thank-you notes can be so effective is the law of reciprocity. There are three key elements to the law of reciprocity, which a handwritten note usually contains:

1. **They are Significant**

    Yes, in a digital, fast paced, get-it-done-now world, a handwritten note makes a statement—the sender took the time to put their thoughts on paper and mail a card.

2. **They are Unexpected**

   Again, in today's world, getting a card that is written and ad-dressed by hand (outside of Christmas time) is typically an unexpected occurrence. Think about the last time you got your mail and found, among all the other "stuff," something handwritten and addressed to you. What got opened first?

3. **They are Personal**

   When done correctly, a handwritten thank-you note is very personal. By done correctly, I mean you take the time to com-pose your thoughts and say, "Thank you" to someone in a meaningful and specific way.

So, to whom could you write a handwritten thank-you card today?

---

Key Takeaways

- Follow through is not the customer's job.

- How you follow through says more about you than all of your marketing colleterial combined.

---

# Chapter Eleven

## Making It Rain

I saved lead generation until late in the book for a reason. I do the same when I'm presenting a training engagement with my consulting clients.

Simply put, why would you want to learn how to generate quality leads without having a solid sales process for navigating a lead or prospect though a professional sales process?

Leads are expensive. If you have the good fortune to work for a company that provides good qualified leads, I can assure you those leads come with a price. I can also assure you someone in the company knows what that price is!

Marketing-generated leads have two costs associated with each one. First is the cost of generating the lead. Social media campaigns, pay-per-click ads, traditional advertising (TV, print and radio) all have a dollar value tied to every choice. I have worked with clients in a wide variety of industries where leads are valued at anywhere from a few dollars apiece to several hundred each.

I worked with one client who knew every inbound phone call cost them, on average, $250. That is a lot of money to make the phone ring!

This leads me to the second cost associated with leads—the missed opportunity cost.

What is the average value in top line sales and bottom line profits to your company? Let's say your company spends $25 per lead to make the phone ring and get a perspective buyer to say, *"Hey, I want to explore doing business with you,"* and, if they do, the average sale will be $2,500, with a 30% profit margin.

That means the profit generated per sale from a lead is $750. How many leads do you have to burn through before you start losing money? In this case the number would be 30. On the surface, this seems reasonable if you average a 30% closing ratio.

So, 100 leads come in and you close 30, or three out of 10. Let's do some more math. 100 leads at $25 each is $2,500. Thirty of those leads result in $75,000 ($2,500 x 30) in top line sales and $22,500 in gross profit.

Not bad, but what happened to the other 75 leads ($1,750 worth)? Did they buy from someone else? Did you lose the sale to no decision? Did they stay with their current provider? It is a question worth asking, and an answer worth knowing.

Those 70 qualified leads have a top line value of $175,000 and $52,500 in gross profit! I am not suggesting you should be at 100%, but I wouldn't be celebrating at 30% either. There are some missed opportunities in this equation.

What would it mean to your book of business if your closing ratio increased by just 5%? I will leave the math to you, or you can refer to the sales metrics from Jill Konrath's book, *Agile Selling*. [10]

**On Your Own**
For those of you who do not have the luxury of a marketing department to generate leads and you must do it yourself, you can and should go through the exercise of knowing the cost of a self-generated lead.

Here is a simple example. If you are a $100,000-a-year earner, that makes every hour of your work life worth $50. A day is worth $400, and a week is worth $2000. This, of course, is based on a five-day work week, at eight hours a day, with two weeks' vacation.

I realize this is not likely to be your personal scenario, but we must start somewhere.

So, if you spend four hours prospecting, you invested $200 of your time to generate a lead. Going to a networking event? That is $100. Surfing LinkedIn for 30 minutes? $25 dollars.

You get the idea. If you are going to invest your time, energy and effort into prospecting, make sure it is worth the investment.

The wiser you invest your time, the higher the return. The higher the return, the more you become worth. The more you are worth, the more money you will make, and, in time, every hour becomes increasingly valuable in terms of your income.

One more way to look at the value of your time is this way. If you write a million dollars' worth of business annually, using the same formula we did for your income, that makes your week worth $20,000, a day worth $4000 and an hour worth $500 to your company. Energy and effort are renewable resources. Time is not.

Sales Professionals know the difference!

## Misconceptions About Prospecting

Few salespeople like prospecting or cold calling. Fewer still actually love it. Interrupting someone, trying to get past a gatekeeper, calling, visiting, even emailing, pinging someone on LinkedIn can all seem like an intrusion.

Hate it, love it or something in between, prospecting is the life blood of a Sales Professional. *"But Les, my firm provides high-quality warm leads. I don't need to prospect."*

Good for you! However, what you're really saying is you are putting your entire career and compensation into someone else's hands.

If you are okay with that, there's no need to read any further. If you don't want to put your career in someone else's hands, there are a few misconceptions about prospecting that need to be cleared up.

The first myth is that prospecting, or cold calling, is limited or exclusive to new organic customers that don't know who you are or what you do. Yes, this is a group that needs to be targeted, but it takes time and energy.

Acquiring brand-new customers is a very expensive and time-consuming task. There are lots of other people you can prospect who can be just as fruitful.

Old customers you or your company lost, and prospects that somehow got into your company's sales cycle and for one reason or another never bought. At one point, these people knew about you or, in the case of lost customers, they trusted you and your company. In other words, these folks aren't easy to get back, but you aren't starting at square one.

The second myth is cold calling doesn't work anymore. This is simply not true. Prospecting requires you to be a professional interrupter, a person who disrupts a prospective customer's day. It's not easy and it isn't much fun, but when done correctly, it is effective.

The last myth I want to dispel is that it's the marketing department's job to generate leads. It's true to a certain extent, but in my opinion the job of marketing is to create awareness and potential interest. It's the job of sales to connect and move that suspect or prospect into the funnel.

That requires the Sales Professional to convert that awareness and possible interest into revenue. That requires prospecting.

### Always Be Prepared!

It amazes me to see salespeople treat cold calls and prospecting calls with less preparation and care than any other call they make. They take short cuts, lack confidence, and mishandle prospecting calls. It's as if they don't value their own time enough to make the most of the effort when prospecting.

Lack of preparation leads to a lack of confidence. Lack of confidence leads to a lack of credibility. Lack of credibility leads to the prospect not being interested in talking to you.

A vicious cycle of the salesperson dreading to make the calls, making them anyway, no matter how poorly, seeing no real results and saying internally *"Well, that was a waste of time."*

A self-fulling prophecy.

A cold call or a prospecting call should be handled with the same level of care and preparation as any other sales call. The same rules in Chapter 4 on preparation apply to prospecting and cold calling.

What is the purpose of your call? What are you trying to accomplish, learn or discover? What do you know? What do you need to know? What do you need them to admit? What questions will you ask? What are the logical next steps?

A cold call or a prospecting call, in order to be effective, requires the same level of care and preparation as the qualifying and discovery calls on a warm lead.

Whether your prospecting efforts are via LinkedIn, email, or even physically visiting a prospect at their place of business, you need to prepare and have something of value to say.

### Nobody answers their phone!
Voicemail is a barrier. It has become the digital version of a gatekeeper. Its sole function? Keeping you out!

This may be a bit of an overstatement, but it sure feels that way some days. Studies have shown that 7.3 out of 10 outbound sales calls end up in voicemail.

As a Sales Professional, you will be hard pressed to change that number. The number you can change is the number of return calls you get. Here are five reasons prospects don't call back:

1. **No clear purpose to your call**

   For starters, let's address the only reason for leaving someone a voicemail ... to get a call back! Start with the end in mind. Just like an actual sales call, you need to have a <u>clear purpose to your call</u>. Most Sales Professionals plan for the actual conversation but fail to plan the voicemail message. You need to plan for both!

   By the way, *"Following up"* or *"Just checking in"* are not clear purposes to a call.

2. **Your message is too long**

   Millions of people are "Delete" keying salespeople out of their lives every day. This is because the message is too long and has no clear purpose. You get less than 30 seconds!

3. **You try and sell on voicemail**

   Remember the only reason to leave a voicemail is to get a call back. Do the selling when you have them engaged in a real conversation.

4. **There is no value in your message**

   I said earlier you have less than 30 seconds before your message gets deleted. I personally shoot for 24 seconds!

   So, in 24 seconds I must say my name and the name of my company, my phone number, state the purpose of my call, grab their *Attention*, create *Interest* and *Desire*, give them a clear call to *Action*, and leave my call back number again slowly.

   Think you can do all of that in less than 30 seconds? It can be done, but only with preparation.

5. **You are unprepared**

   The best way to get your call returned is to use the old marketing strategy AIDA.

   The first "A" is to grab their *Attention*. The "I" stands for *Interest* (this is where you insert value). The "D" stands for *Desire* (more value). Again, this must be about them and what they value not about you! The last "A" stands for *Action*. More specifically, *a call to action.*

When I started my own business, I found myself in need of a financial planner to help me set up an ongoing retirement account. For 15+ years I relied on the HR department of my firm to provide me with retirement options, stock purchase 401k and so on. When I left the corporate world, I needed someone to pick up where I had left off.

Meet Bob! Bob is a certified financial planner and has an impressive list of credentials. Someone I trusted referred him to me, and, after an initial meeting, I was comfortable enough having him set up a new retirement account for me.

During this initial meeting, he indicated he wanted to manage my existing retirement portfolio as well. For a variety of reasons, I was not compelled to move my existing portfolio and politely declined, saying it was not necessary.

Bob, to his credit, called me every three months or so (I suspect because he uses a CRM system to remind him to call me), and, since I travel frequently, I'm a bit hard to get on the phone. As a result, Bob had to leave messages.

His first voicemail message, and each one after that, sounded like this, *"Hi Les. It's Bob. I am just calling to see how things are going. Give me a call when you get a chance."* There were occasional variations of this. Sometimes he would be calling to *"Check in"* or *"Follow up"* or *"Touch base."*

Each message had no real purpose (that I was aware of) or any value to me. I was sure the purpose of his call was to talk about the old retirement portfolio and how he would like to manage it, but, alas, his messages never created any interest and, as a result, I never returned his calls. Not because I didn't like him, but because I (just like your prospects, customers, and clients) have stuff going on. Stuff that gets prioritized and stuff that gets dismissed as unimportant.

One afternoon I was at my desk and Bob gets me live! We had a terrific conversation. He was prepared and had information I was missing. At the end of the call, I had agreed to move the balance of my retirement portfolio to him. We were both happy.

As the call started to wind down, Bob asked me if I would answer a personal question. When I agreed, he asked, *"I've been calling you every three months like clockwork trying to share this information with you. So, my question is why didn't you return my calls?"*

Feeling comfortable with Bob, I asked if he was ready to hear some tough feedback. Laughing, he said, *"Yeah. Let me hear it!"*

I said, *"Bob, your voicemails suck!"*

I went on to walk him through the same methodology from point #4 of this chapter about stating his name and number, the purpose of his call and the AIDA components of a well planned and executed voicemail. After listening to me for a few minutes, he replied, *"That all sounds great in theory, but I don't believe it can all be done in less than 30 seconds."*

I said, *"Give me a minute to prepare and I'll give you an example."* When I was ready, I said, *"Okay, time me."* Bob chuckled and said, *"Okay, go."*

"Les, it's Bob from ABC Financial (800) 555-1234. The reason I am calling is I have been reviewing your retirement portfolio like I do every month (Attention), and there are some things going on in the marketplace you should know about (Interest). I think we can accelerate your rate of return (Desire). Please give me a call today at (800) 555-1234, I am at my desk until 4:30 pm (Call to Action)."

When I finished, Bob let me know it took less than 30 seconds. Less than 30 seconds to execute, and only a few minutes of planning.

Now, there is no guarantee a message like this will get your call returned, but at the very least it lets your prospect, customer, or client know you are not going to waste their time, and, at the most, it should improve your call back rates.

At the beginning of my consulting career, I got very good at leaving messages. I got good at it by following this process, and practicing. I would write out my voice mail message, edit the message ruthlessly, say it out loud several times and time the message. Then I would record the message on my own voicemail and listen to what they would hear.

I put this to the test when I was challenged by my first business partner to call hundreds of prospects in our data base to sell tickets to our workshops. Moving though the data base smoothly and efficiently leaving professional messages at a crisp pace. I got so comfortable getting peoples voicemail and leaving messages that, when I got a real human voice after about 20 calls, I froze for an instant!

**Prospect:** *"Hello, this is Dave."*

**Me:** *"Uh..."*

**Dave:** *"Yes?"*

**Me:** *"Sorry about that, Dave. I was expecting your voicemail."*

**Dave:** *"If you want, I'll hang up and you can call back. Then you'll get my voicemail."*

My point is plan for the call if you do connect, and plan for the voicemail if you don't.

# REALITY CHECK:
## A Matter of Trust

I had a coaching session with a client of mine who was struggling to get anywhere in the cold calling process. He turned to me and said, "All of these guys are either lying or going out of business!"

He was calling on contractors most likely to need and buy his product, and after a brief introduction to himself and his company, he would ask, "Do you have any projects you would like me to quote for you?" The response was always "No."

My client assumed all of these people were lying or going out of business. After all, how could they stay in business if they weren't involved in any projects?

The truth was the contractors were answering a different question. The real answer was they didn't have anything for *him* to quote because they didn't know, like or trust him... yet.

This prompted a change in strategy. My client started focusing on "connecting" with them on a professional level--asking questions about their business, their current challenges, what types of projects they preferred doing, etc. By changing his initial approach and making it about them first, he started getting prospects to say, "I have a couple things coming up. Can you get me some pricing?"

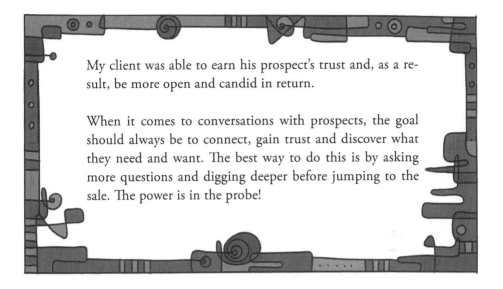

My client was able to earn his prospect's trust and, as a result, be more open and candid in return.

When it comes to conversations with prospects, the goal should always be to connect, gain trust and discover what they need and want. The best way to do this is by asking more questions and digging deeper before jumping to the sale. The power is in the probe!

## Know to Whom You Need to Talk!

As you navigate the sales cycle (from prospecting to closing the deal), you will encounter several types of people along the way. Knowing who they are and their role in the process is critical to your success.

### Information Gatherers

This person is doing exactly that—gathering information about your product or service. If it is a marketing-generated lead, they are probably gathering information from your competition too!

Follow through here is critical—time is not your friend! The key here is providing the information requested and gathering some of your own, such as timeline, sense of urgency, current situation etc.

### Influencers

These folks are critical to the process. They come in many forms and from many areas inside the four walls of your prospect's organization. They can come from *Operations*, *Finance*, and *Executive Staff* to name just a few.

Understand who they are and how your offering affects them. It will be important to speak their language, too. *Finance* cares about ROI, *Operations* about ease of use and integration, and CEOs usually just want things done!

## End Users

These are the people who will actually use your product or service. It does not necessarily mean they are part of the buying process, but they could be. How does your product or service impact them?

## Decision Makers

This is where the rubber meets the road. Decision makers can be challenging to get in front of. They usually live at the top of an organization and place a high premium on their time—so do not waste it!

They rely on input from all the folks I have listed above, but it is their call. They may not be the person using your product or service directly, but they will own the decision to buy from you and the consequences—good or bad.

At the risk of stating the obvious, an individual could represent more than one, or all, of the roles mentioned above. The key is being able to address the needs and concerns of each role.

You might want to read the book *Mastering the Complex Sale* by Jeff Thull to learn more about the myth of the sole decision maker.[11]

### A Few Words About "Gatekeepers"

I am frequently asked, *"How do I get past the gatekeeper"?* My standard reply, *"Stop calling them that"!* The term is out-of-date and disrespectful.

The way you address and treat the first people you encounter will determine whether you get to meet anyone else! It is important to note the people tasked with protecting the assets (time and money) of real decision makers, aka "gatekeepers," usually take on the role of "information gatherer" and often "influencer." Depending on what you sell, they could also be "end users."

Get their name and use it as soon as possible. Your goal is to demonstrate to them you are worthy of the boss' time. They should be your first sale and the thing you are selling is you!

Working in the field with a salesperson who represented a client several years ago, we were cold calling on district offices of major school districts. The purpose of his call was to secure the name of the person responsible for making decisions about maintenance issues at the district level.

My client provided a service that was highly regulated and required by every school, public and private. The calls we were making were more information gathering. The people we needed to speak with were not easy to track down and, at the time, not typical users of LinkedIn or participants in networking events. In short, we needed to hunt them down, and the most logical place was the district office.

The seller I was working with had a good opening statement and clear purpose to his call. In less than three hours, we had called on six school districts, and at each call our first point of contact was siting just inside the front door behind a desk. If you have been in similar situations, you may imagine this would be the gatekeeper, and with that attitude you would be correct.

Don't me wrong; we encounter someone in an administrative role on every call. Each has a nameplate with titles like *Receptionist, Administrator,* and even *Secretary* and, of course, their name. The salesperson I was coaching that day greeted each person with his name, the name of his company and the purpose of his call. In every case he got some information but rarely all the information he needed or required to really advance the sales cycle.

During our end-of-day debrief, to prove a point, I asked him if he knew the name of the first person we met. He did not (for the record, it was Betty.) I asked if he knew the name of the second person we met. He did not—I told him it was Sue. We did this for each call, and every time he did not know the person's name.

I explained to him that the reason I remembered, and he didn't, was simple. Each person had a nameplate with his or her name on it—an opportunity to use the person's name. If they didn't have a nameplate, the easiest option would have been to ask, then use their name throughout the conversation. This may sound like a blinding flash of the obvious, but I can assure you this is missed far too often.

### Lost or Prior Customers

In the introduction to this book, I defined the differences between suspects, prospects, customers, clients, advocates, and confidants.

Sales Professionals value their clients more than anything else. That being said, on occasion we all lose good clients. Sometimes we lose them through no fault of our own. I call lost clients "away clients."

Sometimes they move away, sometimes they pass away (or go out of business and close), sometimes they get pushed away. Make no mistake, you will lose clients. As a percentage, it should be somewhere in the single digits, like less than 5%. If they close their business, or move away, there is not much you can do. But the number one reason we lose clients is perceived *indifference*.

Their perception is you as their Sales Professional have become indifferent to *their* current needs, pains, fears, and desires. As in life, stuff happens in business. It is very easy to take a good or great client for granted. We don't do it deliberately, but sometimes we can take strong relationships for granted.

When we take them for granted, we put them at risk. When we put a relationship at risk by overestimating our relationship, we open the door for competitors.

Working with the sales professions and salespeople as a sales coach, I have heard the following phrases far too often when they describe the nature of the relationship they have with a customer, or client: *"Oh, that's Bob at ABC Company. He loves me."* or *"They love me."* It has been my experience this can mark the first stage of failure for some relationships.

Let's examine the statement a bit further. They love you? No, they don't! They love their spouses, their kids, and their families, but it is not likely they feel the same way about you, their Sales Professional. When I hear those types of statements, I will often push back immediately. *"Love you!?! They don't love you, they love their family. Right now, they are not even thinking about you!"*

They may like you and trust you, but when we make statements like they love us, we are at risk of taking them and their needs for granted. As a best practice, it is highly recommended you use the Sales Professional Pyramid Model to conduct periodic business reviews with your best customers and clients. Think in terms of reconnecting, rediscovering, and reengaging. When things change in your client's world you are at risk of them changing in yours.

## The Best Source of All
The absolute best source of self-generated leads come from referrals. As a Sales Professional, when you do your job right, meaning you have not only met your prospect, customer or client's expectations, you've exceeded it, you've earned the right to ask for a referral. Make no mistake; when you do your job well, it shouldn't be a surprise when your best customer or client gives you a referral. But why wait? If you were to look at your past and current list of customers and clients, it's likely many of them not only know people who would benefit from doing business with you, they'd also want to make an introduction if you were to ask.

Like so many things about the sales process, this too seems pretty simple. And it is. But, like so many other things about sales, it's not always easy. There are two specific rules I would like to share with you about asking for referrals. `

## Rule #1 Only ask for a referral, once you have earned the right to do so!
There are all kinds of indicators you've earned the right. Perhaps they tell you directly how much they have enjoyed working with you or benefited from the product or service you provided. If this hasn't happened, don't be afraid to ask how the experience was. The point is knowing the best time to ask is when they have had a favorable experience.

## Rule #2 No Short Cuts!

The reasons referrals are so valuable is they have a much higher likelihood of closing. The reason for this is they are likely already qualified, and because someone made the referral, the referee is far more likely to take your call and listen to what you have to say. Lots of good stuff here, but it can all go sideways if we take short cuts in the Connection, Motivation, and overall discovery process.

If you need a solid script and plan for how to asks for referrals, check out *Exactly What to Say*, by Phil Jones.[12] In this excellent follow up to his book Magic Words, Jones details a solid process for generating high quality and receptive leads via referrals.

## Key Takeaways

- If you really want to control your destiny as a Sales Professional, you'll need to make your own rain.

- Prospecting and lead generation are the life blood of a true Sales Professional.

- Prospecting calls must be handled with the same level of care and planning as every other call.

- Referrals are your best source of new business.

# Chapter Twelve

## The Power Of The Playbook

I travel a lot, and as a result, I spend a lot of time in airports.

On one occasion, I met a couple of pilots waiting in line at the coffee stand in my home airport. Under their arm were there caps or hats. You may have seen these official looking billed hats yourself. Similar to the cap a city policeman might wear.

I noticed one of the pilots had a gold leaf stitched on the bill of his hat and the other pilot's hat did not. Curious, I asked what the embroidery signified. *"Oh, that means I have over 10,000 hours of flight time."*

Impressive, I thought, 10,000 hours. If you've ever read Malcolm Gladwell's book *Outliers*, you are likely familiar with the concept of 10,000 hours of practice or experience is the time most associated with achieving mastery of something. 10,000 hours of flight time to me must mean he had mastery in piloting. [13]

So, I asked, *"You probably don't need to use a preflight checklist any more with all of those hours?"* His response was, *"No, I use a checklist every time. Always."*

I was relieved to hear this, realizing he might be the pilot of the plane I was about to board.

Of course, he uses a checklist! Lives are at stake. Lots of things can go wrong. The checklist is the tool used to ensure everyone's safety and well-being.

Most sales organizations don't have a Sales Playbook, the equivalent of the pilot's checklist. While it's unlikely that not having a Playbook won't cost any lives during a sale, you do run the risk of killing the sale from poor planning.

## The Hard Facts

Less than 25% of companies have a Sales Playbook or defined sales process—a checklist for how to handle sales. More startling is compared to their peer group, in organizations with an effective sales process:

- *Average win rates are 31% higher*

- *21% more salespeople achieve quota*

- *Company-wide revenue performance is 17% higher*

If you are not meeting your potential, you have question marks about your salespeople, or you are not sure if they are doing the right things, the first place to start would be to build a Sales Playbook.

Sales Playbooks should provide your sales team with guidance, direction, and a process designed to take a prospect through the entire sales process from initial lead generation to revenue generation!

At the risk of being too granular, here are some things your Playbook should include:

## Who Do We Sell To and What Do We Sell?

Start by defining who your ideal customers are. A customer profile should list the industries you sell into, the title(s) of who is involved in the entire sales process, their roles, and responsibilities.

From there you can start to capture the problems they face that your product or service solves and the benefits they get by doing business with you. You might be surprised if you knew how many leads and prospects your people chase that should never be pursued to begin with!

Simply put, your playbook should include a list of whom you sell to and whom you do not.

## What Do You Have to Know?

Once you are clear on who your customers truly are, you can create a list of the things your sales team needs to know about the prospect and their company. Don't take for granted they know what they need to know!

Your list of "need to know" items can include everything from the painfully obvious like the correct spelling and pronunciation of the prospect's name to the sublime like what are they trying to accomplish and why it is important to them?

Here is a fun exercise: Gather your sales team or colleagues together and brainstorm a list of these "need to know" items about the person, the company, their situation, and get as detailed as you can.

The list can easily dip into the three figures. Now ask your best people to think about their best clients and ask how many of the things they can answer!

## What to Look For?

Now that you are armed with a list of things to know, you can enhance your Playbook by creating a list of things to look out for.

**What should they be looking for before the sales call?**

- *Website*

- *LinkedIn Profile(s)*

- *Press releases*

- *News articles*

**What should they be looking for during the sales call?**

Clues in and around the building, such as…

- *Traffic*

- *Cleanliness*

- *Employee morale*

- *What they measure publicly*

- *What they are most proud of*

- *The level of engagement by stakeholders*

- *Questions they ask*

## What Should You be Asking?

Armed with your first two lists, you can craft a list of specific questions your team needs to ask to navigate the prospect successfully through the sales cycle. Using the two previous lists will make the process of creating questions easier.

What questions will you need to ask to establish a strong connection, discover their motivations, their needs, and arm yourself with the information needed to present a strong value proposition?

Going through the exercises above, particularly with your current team, will go a long way to building a duplicable and professional sales process.

# REALITY CHECK:
## Playbook = Better Closing Ratios

The first Sales Playbook I built with a client was a simple affair—a single page printed front and back.

It opened with the salesperson making their opening statement and outlining the steps of the sale from start to finish, with a few questions on each section and a place to capture the answers. A road map to helping navigate the prospect from the start of the sales call to its logical conclusion.

When it was finished and rolled out, there were two metrics that had an immediate positive impact. The first was the duration of the sales calls. Prior to the Playbook, the average sales call took just over an hour. Once the Playbook was adopted, the sales calls started averaging 45 to 50 minutes in length.

Having a plan sped things up—it didn't slow them down.

The second more powerful metric or measure of effectiveness was a significant increase in closing ratio—the ratio of total opportunities in the pipeline to the number of "won" opportunities.

Prior to the creation, roll out and adoption of the new Sales Playbook, the closing ratio for this client averaged 26%. For every 100 qualified opportunities the marketing team generated only 26 closed and generated revenue. Within a month of using the Playbook, the closing ratio jumped to 34%!

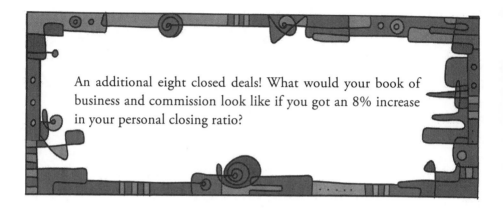

An additional eight closed deals! What would your book of business and commission look like if you got an 8% increase in your personal closing ratio?

## Key Takeaways

- Playbooks are your checklist for ensuring the highest probability of success.

- Less than 25% of companies in the US have a formal Sales Playbook. This is what you are competing against.

# Endnotes

## Introduction

[1] Layo, Gerry. *Smart Selling: Strategies To Reinvent The Sales Process*. La Jolla: PSCI Publishing, 2003. Print.

[2] Wickman, Gino. *Traction: Get A Grip On Your Business*. Dallas: BenBella Books, 2011. Print.

## Chapter 1

[3] Pink, Daniel. *To Sell Is Human: The Surprising Truth About Moving Others*. New York: Penguin, 2012. Print.

[4] Blount, Jeb. *Objections: The Art and Science of Getting Past No*. Hoboken: Wiley & Sons, 2018. Print.

## Chapter 6

[5] Thomas, George J. and Jenkins, Jerry B. *Verbal Judo: The Gentle Art Of Persuasion*. New York: HarperCollins, 2013. Print.

[6] *Verbal Judo*

## Chapter 8

[7] Fox, Jeffrey J. *How To Become A Rainmaker: The Rules For Getting And Keeping Customers And Clients*. New York: Hyperion, 2000. Print.

## Chapter 9

[8] Gitomer, Jeffrey. *The Little Red Book Of Selling: 12.5 Principles Of Sales Greatness*. China: R.R. Donnelley, 2004. Print.

[9] Iannarion, Anthony. *The Lost Art of Closing: Winning the Ten Commitments That Drive Sales*. New York: Portfolio/Penguin, 2017. Print.

## Chapter 11
[10] Konrath, Jill. *Agile Selling: Get Up To Speed Quickly In Today's Ever-Changing Sales World*. New York: Portfolio/Penguin, 2014. Print.

[11] Thull, Jeff. *Mastering the Complex Sale*. 2nd Edition. Hoboken: Wiley & Sons, 2010. Print.

[12] Jones, Phil M. *Exactly What to Say: The Magic Words for Influence and Impact*. Hoboken: Box of Tricks, 2017. Print.

## Chapter 12
[13] Gladwell, Malcolm. *Outliers: The Story Of Success*. New York: Little, Brown & Company, 2008. Print.

Made in the USA
Columbia, SC
04 August 2019